MULTICULTURAL
PSYCHOLOGY AN
Series Editors: Allen E. Iv

Multicultural Encounters:
Case Narratives from a Counseling Practice
Stephen Murphy-Shigematsu

Community Genograms:
Using Individual, Family, and Cultural Narratives with Clients
Sandra A. Rigazio-DiGilio, Allen E. Ivey,
Lois T. Grady, and Kara P. Kunkler-Peck

Learning from My Mother's Voice:
Family Legend and the Chinese American Experience
Jean Lau Chin

My mother and Sel Ming at the age of 5 in Nanjing just before she left him for the United States. Also pictured are Dai Q (her brother) and his family, Ah Gung (her father), stepmother, and half-sister Ah Yee. This was the only family picture my mother had.

Learning from My Mother's Voice

Family Legend and the Chinese American Experience

Jean Lau Chin

Foreword by Jessica Henderson Daniel

Teachers College, Columbia University
New York and London

In honor of my mother, Fung Gor Lee.
Dedicated to my parents, my family, and my children.
In celebration of those before us, to those with us, and for those after us
toward our bonds with one another.

Published by Teachers College Press, 1234 Amsterdam Avenue, New York, NY 10027

Copyright © 2005 by Teachers College, Columbia University

Library of Congress Cataloging-in-Publication Data

Chin, Jean Lau.
  Learning from my mother's voice: family legend & the Chinese American experience / foreword by Jessica Henderson Daniel.
    p. cm.— (Multicultural foundations of psychology and counseling)
  Includes bibliographical references and index.
  ISBN 0-8077-4552-9 (acid-free paper) — ISBN 0-8077-4551-0 (acid-free paper: pbk.)
    1. Chinese American families. 2. Chinese American women. 3. Storytelling—Psychological aspects. 4. Mythology, Chinese. 5. Chin, Jean Lau. I. Title. II. Series.

E184.C5C4735 2005
305.898'1073—dc22   2004062055

ISBN 0-8077-4551-0 (paper)
ISBN 0-8077-4552-9 (cloth)

Printed on acid-free paper
Manufactured in the United States of America

12 11 10 09 08 07 06 05   8 7 6 5 4 3 2 1

Contents

Foreword

The very title of Jean Lau Chin's book—*Learning from My Mother's Voice*—both honors her mother, a courageous woman who immigrated to the United States from China, and indicates her mother's primary role within the text as she describes life both in China and in the United States, as well as her own immigration journey. It is a tribute to her mother and other women who experienced immigration then and now.

Examining the life of one's mother often means the exploration of geography (i.e., place), time period, and people central to her life. It can also mean learning about socialization through literature, particularly mythology and storytelling. In the case of the former, one is limited only by the imaginations of the storyteller and the listener. Stories can address racial and/or ethnic geography (see Frankenberg, 1993) and gender geography—that is, the particular people who occupy those physical spaces (see Lightfoot, 1988; Wade-Gayles, 1993; Walker, 1983). In this book, the reader is carried through history and time to varied locations and across several generations through mythology and storytelling that is focused on the lives of Chinese women.

As the reader takes Jean Lau Chin's guided tours through myth and cultural history, it is clear that these stories are more than entertainment: They represent cultural messages about living as a woman. The juxtaposition of Chinese and Western myths with their similarities and differences, followed by the author's incisive analysis of contemporary stories depicting Asian women in print and on the screen, provide culturally driven connections to perceptions and behaviors of Chinese women both individually and in relation to the world. Through these stories, a rich tapestry of information about Chinese women and Chinese American women emerges. The stereotypical Chinese woman fails to appear as the various lenses of ethnicity, gender, location, and epoch make explicit the diversity that exists within any ethnic group and liberate us by providing an informed array of images and possibilities.

These stories and myths give us context for the voice of Fung Gor

Lee, the author's mother. Her autobiography—detailed in a first-person narrative in Chapters 4 and 5 of this book—is given additional meaning and depth when readers are made aware of the literature and myths that shaped not only the perceptions and experiences of Mrs. Lee, but also their own. Here, storytelling takes on new dimensions for the reader and the writer.

Despite daughter and mother living in very different daily worlds, the strong, viable connection maintained between them, as well as their lived stories, confirm that difference does not justify disconnection. Further, telling one's story in cultural context can be a healing experience and an affirmation of worth and value. Through storytelling, mythology, and autobiography, Jean Lau Chin has asserted that her mother's life will continue to matter.

—Jessica Henderson Daniel

REFERENCES

Frankenberg, R. (1993). *White women, race matters.* Minneapolis, MN: University of Minnesota Press.

Lightfoot, S. L. (1988). *Balm in Gilead.* Reading, MA: Addison-Wesley.

Wade-Gayles,G. (1993). *Pushed back to strength.* Boston, MA: Beacon Press.

Walker, A. (1983). *In search of our mothers' gardens.* New York: Harcourt, Brace & Jovanovich.

Introduction

Storytelling has been popular through the ages as a way of capturing the meaning and essence of the human condition. Conflicts and problem solving, hopes and dreams, losses and trauma, described through legend and myth have captured and enraptured those through the generations who find commonality with a given plight. Storytelling has served as the emotional bridge between storyteller and listener and provided a therapeutic atmosphere for healing among its listeners. The transformation of the self, often described as a journey through the use of saga, myth, and legend, has enabled listeners and observers to participate and connect across generations and cultures. Cultural legends nurture and sustain those who listen; they describe the cycle of life and enable listeners to connect with their roots and resolve unsolved life dilemmas.

All immigrant families have sagas about their immigration journey, which include their dreams, disappointments, and frustrations. These sagas describe the developmental tasks of adapting to a new environment, dealing with daily living, and surviving in an alien culture. They also describe the life cycle, beginning with one's creation, progressing to the journey taken in life, ending with the transformation of self toward enlightenment. These sagas become the legends and myths that not only bond us through the generations with the connections we form, but also put us in a type of bondage, as immigrant families are unable to step outside their stories of survival, suffering, and hardship. All immigrant families share a dream for a better life. It is out of this dream that legends are created. I speak of the "immigration legend" that all immigrant families create, and of the intergenerational bonds that help to create them, which are found in all cultures—bonds of creation, between women, between mothers and sons, between mothers and daughters, and between generations of families.

The myths and legends rooted in our native cultures provide the impetus for creating these immigration legends. Nothing captures the journey of Chinese immigration better than *Journey to the West,* a classic Chinese epic symbolizing the search for enlightenment by its hero, Monkey King, a smart but rebellious character who needed to face 81 dangers before he achieved enlightenment.

Whereas Eastern and Western worldviews are often in stark contrast to one another, the Chinese legends and myths remembered by Chinese American immigrant families will also be transformed by the influence of Western culture and by the passing of time. When East is West, opposing worldviews between Chinese and American cultures challenge the development of identity; Chinese Americans often need to dichotomize cultural realities since it is not possible to create a logical integration of two opposing views.

Mythology and storytelling have captured the imagination and meaning of life for generations—they speak of creation, rebirth, interpersonal and family bonds, and the journey of life. They provide answers to questions about the cycle of life.

Storytelling is often captured in the fairy tales of a culture. Each culture has had its own set of stories and legends that sustain its people and nurture its children. As groups immigrate to other lands, they cherish these stories and legends while creating new ones of their immigration experience. These immigration legends that emerge nurture and sustain immigrant families as they make their journey in new and different cultures.

Part I of this book is about Chinese mythology and the stories about creation, women, bonds, and the journey to enlightenment, which are themes about the cycle of life. As we examine the stories, we can see the themes in Chinese mythology mirrored in the life experiences of Chinese American immigrants. Life is a journey, and the immigrant experience highlights that journey with the added challenge of being uprooted and transplanted to a new and different culture. This book argues that as immigrants make this journey, they create new stories and legends about the cycle of life to help sustain them and nurture their children. These new legends become part of a group's identity.

As immigrants become assimilated into the culture of the United States, their children and future generations may lose touch with the struggle and striving of their immigrant forebears and forget the almost daily challenges to their survival. Waves of immigrants to the United States have changed through the generations; they come from different countries; the contexts compelling them to migrate differ; however, the psychological issues faced by all immigrants remain very similar. Each immigrant group should consciously create its own immigration legends—each needs to tell its story and create its new identity.

Drawing on the themes in Chinese mythology, this book examines psychological themes of separation, loss, and guilt, and discusses how pervasive they are in the lives and adjustments of Chinese American immigrant families. While the journey of immigration is a quest for freedom, there is also loss—that of family, culture, and homeland. Immigrants often cling to the symbols and myths of their culture in order to restore what was lost; in doing so, they experience the bonds and bondage of being Chinese American. The bonds of a shared culture and the connections with family and community promote resiliency and happiness. At the same time, the obligations of family prescribed by culture and guilt over abandoning family and culture as a result of immigration creates a bond that often lasts a lifetime. While many Chinese American immigrants succeeded in their quest to leave China for a better life, many were never able to leave the Chinatowns in America.

The values of Chinese culture can be found in its symbols. Consequently, an examination of symbols in Chinese culture, both contemporary and historical, can help to illustrate how Chinese cultural values provide the bondage that hold families and communities together; but it also shows the bonds that hold them back. Contrasting Chinese and American cultural symbols also illustrate the challenges that Chinese Americans face in creating their new identity and in adapting to a new culture. As Chinese immigrant families attempt to assimilate into American society, a culture vastly different in its legends, myths, and symbols, they need to create a bicultural identity if they are to retain their sense of self-esteem and belongingness.

In Part II of this book, oral history is used: A family saga describes an immigration journey for one Chinese American family. The influence of mythology and cultural symbols in the daily life of this family illustrates how it lives Chinese culture and uses Chinese legends and stories to nurture and sustain its growth. A comparison of historical and sociopolitical events between China and the United States at the beginning of the 20th century sets the context for this saga and enriches the bicultural symbolism and mythology that unfold in the oral history.

The themes of promise and obligation, loss and abandonment guilt, poverty and survival, ritual and sacrifice, and pride and respect, spoken through the voice of a Chinese mother, captures the experiences of many Chinese American immigrant families. The oral history is a story of:

- Intergenerational bonds
- Mothers and daughters
- Survival and striving

- Women, family, and culture
- Chinese American immigrants.

It is narrated by my mother, Fung Gor Lee, and written by me. The poems introducing each chapter are written by her granddaughter and my niece, Tracey Lynette Ong. The oral history is set in a historical context that spans events of more than a century: from the gold rush in California during the 1850s, to the Japanese invasion of China (1930s), through World War II (1940s), to the political ideology of communism in China and McCarthyism (1950s), to the civil rights and the women's movements in the United States (1960s). These events were the trials and tests of forbearance faced by Toisanese immigrants in their journey to the West. Toisanese immigrants from the Canton Province of China were the earliest Chinese immigrants, and now make up the fabric of most second- and third-generation Chinese in the United States. The need for cheap labor in the United States, coupled with devastating floods in Canton, China, led to the heavy immigration of Chinese men. At the same time, restrictive and discriminatory anti-Chinese legislation heavily influenced patterns of immigration where husbands remained separated from wives and families for years, even decades.

Lest future generations lose touch with the immigrant experience of their forebears, the creation of immigration legend is discussed in Part III. This is both a process and a product. It is a process for families to preserve for future generations what may be forgotten, and to revisit their ancestry through cultural mythology and family saga. It is a process for families to create intergenerational bonds in order to provide hope for the future and restore faith in the present. It is a process for counselors working with immigrant families to apply storytelling techniques and to draw on cultural mythology and symbols to promote the transformation of their clients in their journey to reduce the bondage and expand the bonds of family and culture. In any process, the task is one of self-reflection.

Finally, the products are the lessons to be learned in living out one's family saga and creating the immigration legends and cultural mythology. The saga of surviving and striving day by day should resonate not only with Chinese Americans, but also with all Americans who have immigrant roots. Despite the global economy of the 21st century and instant internet access to the far corners of the world, changes that make our world vastly different from the 20th century, the psychological themes of acculturation remain constant. Our connections with the past are still an important part of the journey that all immigrants must make to achieve a bicultural identity.

Part I

Family Saga and Cultural Legend

The presentation of Chinese mythology and legends is intended to offer an Eastern worldview, and to demonstrate how it is used in the daily struggle, survival, and adaptation among Chinese American immigrant families. Chinese American families draw on these legends as examples of how to conduct themselves socially and morally, as sources of solace for coping with a hostile host environment, and as comforting reminders of their identity and connections with the culture they left behind. The mythology and legends are a statement of difference as well as one of common bonding. For Chinese women whose history and contributions were often subordinated to men, the Woman Warrior, both its classic and contemporary versions, captures the strength and resiliency of women in male-dominated cultures.

Cultural values are also embodied in our cultural symbols. Given that Chinese culture stresses the use of metaphors and symbolism, food and words become highly symbolic in capturing the essence of the culture and its values. This is best embodied in the traditional Chinese banquet, which is full of ritual and decorum—intended to demonstrate abundance by the number and quality of dishes, generosity of its host, harmony and balance in the choice of dishes, and bonding in its execution and decorum.

Finally, there is a parallel between the personal saga and the sociohistorical saga, each enriching the other. The creation of personal and family legend is often aligned with the sociohistorical past and context of the present. As Chinese American immigrants salvage the vestiges of culture in their legends, myths, and stories and bring them along on their journey to the West, these are transformed by the social and political events of the present. World War II, communism in China, and the civil rights movement are but some of the events that Chinese immigrants have used to build their new cultural identity and to create their immigration legends.

Chapter 1

Mythology and Storytelling: Of Women, Family, and Culture

Just a Matter of Time

Time gives you the chance to think things out
Things you've missed but will some day endure.
Time gives you a sense of thought,
that only you know deep down
And will keep to yourself.

Times like these are times we all cherish,
They give us the chance to really believe
in ourselves, our dreams, and our goals.
Such precious moments are...
Just a matter of time.

Tracey Lynette Ong

CREATION MYTHS: IN THE BEGINNING

According to Genesis (The Holy Bible, 1999) in Western culture,

> In the beginning God created the heavens and the earth. . . .God created man in the image of Himself; in the image of God He created them; male

and female he created them....God planted a garden of Eden, which is in the east, and there he put the man he had fashioned....You may eat indeed of all the trees in the garden. Nevertheless of the tree of the knowledge of good and evil, you are not to eat, for on the day you eat of it you shall most surely die....[Not having found a suitable helpmate for man, God] made man fall into a deep sleep. And while he slept, he took one of the ribs and enclosed it in flesh...into a woman, and brought her to the man.

In contrast, the Chinese creation myth, which is similar in many Asian cultures, says that at the beginning of time, all was chaos:

Chaos was shaped like a hen's egg. The parts of the egg separated into the Yin and the Yang, the male and female essences of all living things. The lighter parts rose to the top, becoming sky and heaven, while the heavier parts sank to become the earth and sea. The opposing tendencies of male and female are in each of us. (Bierlein, 1994, pp. 53, 73)

All cultures have their creation myths. These myths provide the lens to our culture; they provide us with the models for human behavior that give meaning and value to life. They give symbolic expression to a transition process, or rite of passage, such as a metaphoric death of an old, inadequate self that is reborn on a higher plane of existence. Two differences between fairy tales and myths, however, are worth emphasizing. Myths generally convey something absolutely unique, often grandiose and supernatural. Fairy tales, by contrast, are often unusual and improbable but are presented as ordinary. A second major difference is that the story endings in myths are nearly always tragic, while they are almost always happy in fairy tales (Bettelheim, 1976).

Yin and Yang: Gender Roles

From the beginning, the creation myths in Western and Asian cultures give rise to different images of men and women and messages about gender roles. In contrast to the male dominance of the biblical creation myth of the West, the Chinese myth emphasizes the duality of gender in each of us. It is the opposing tendencies between yin and yang, and the balance between the two, that is essential in the universe. Although variations of these themes will be found in all cultures such that we might say there are more commonalities among us than differences, it is the differences that make each individual culture unique and have persisted through the generations.

The relationship between Eve and the serpent in the Bible summarizes the exclusion of women from knowledge and power. Eve, or woman, represents the desire, transgression, and shame that Adam, or man, must repress. God formulates the code of eroticism between the sexes as though it were a code of war; that is, "I will put enmity between thee and woman, and between thy seed and her seed" (Kristeva, 1986, p. 21).

Creation Myth of Immigration: Rebirth

In Chinese American history, it is the men we hear about as the warriors and conquerors. It is the men we hear about as the pioneers, and as the ones who built the railroads. Yet it has been the women, in their roles as caretakers, as mothers, and as matriarchs, who have helped to heal and grapple with the loss, trauma, and rebirth inherent in the immigration experience. It has been the women who have re-created the psychological environment and community networks so comfortable and reminiscent of home. Women's connectedness—as the bearers of children and culture—have been the anchors in Chinese American families; their roles have been unsung until of late, often subsumed behind the stature of their men and husbands. These are the stories written by men.

There is a creation myth embedded in the immigration story; immigration is a rebirth as families start afresh. As women retell these stories, we can see early Chinese American immigrant women who toiled with their men in laundries and restaurants as they performed their unique roles of psychological healing and emotional bonding. The yin and yang of Chinese mythology reinforces the duality of gender in each of us. Given the scarcity of Chinese women in America at the beginning of the 20th century, they helped to unify and recreate family through their cooking, caretaking, and healing. They maintained their bonds with family members remaining in China through letter writing that instructed, consoled, and connected—unlike today's instant global internet communications. These roles have been largely marginalized as unprofessional and unworthy of literary acclaim. Since women were relegated to the home, their roles have been viewed as "not out in the real world" compared to the roles of men as breadwinners. They struggled to be different as much as they struggled to be the same. In so doing, they created a new world, a bicultural one, in the image of the old, for their families here in America.

MYTHS OF WOMEN

In looking at myths through the ages, Bachofen, a Swiss scholar of the Greek classics, came to the conclusion that there were three clear stages in early European culture. The first was a barbaric stage, followed by a matriarchy that, in turn, was supplanted by a patriarchy. In the barbaric stage, neither male nor female were dominant in society, resulting in widespread sexual promiscuity when children did not know their fathers, women were defenseless, and family life was virtually nonexistent. Aphrodite, the Greek goddess of love, characterized this period.

Next, women banded together for their own defense, leading to the development of a matriarchal society, reflected in the Greek myths of Amazons and fierce woman warriors. The nurturing aspect of femalehood was symbolized by Demeter, goddess of the crops in love of the mother and worship of a mother goddess. Revival of these matriarchal themes and images was seen in the contemporary TV series *Xena*, featuring a female Greek warrior who combines the two faces of womanhood. Xena is a savior through her warrior conquests against the best of men. Unlike many popular heroes, her character is not pure or innocent; her bad side is suggested by past deeds of an evil nature. But her loyalty and sisterhood to Gabrielle symbolize the pure, unadulterated innocence of femalehood.

Bachofen interpreted the myth of Oedipus as the depiction of the three phases of this struggle. Oedipus kills the Sphinx, symbol of hermaphroditic characteristics. He then marries his mother, ruler of Thebes. Her downfall was interpreted as a transition from matriarchy to patriarchy (Bierlein, 1994).

Bachofen's theory about European culture has its parallel in Chinese history and Asian culture. According to Kristeva (1986), a matriarchy derived from peasant origins preceded the patriarchal Confucian family in China; this revolution in the rules of kinship can be traced to sometime around 1000 B.C. In China, this shift to a patriarchy preserved more elements from the earlier matriarchy than its counterpart in European culture. Kristeva hypothesizes that this was due to the extraordinarily advanced development of the matrilineal family in China.

One Chinese myth that mixes history with legend speaks to the existence of this age. Suffering from the big flood of the Yellow River, Yu the Great (2198 B.C.) organizes the lands and waters by causing the Yellow River to flow when he opens the Dragon's Gate. According to legend, his creation dance used to tame the waters imitated a feminine form as a symbol of the political authority. When he is caught dancing by his wife, he kills her and turns her to stone, thus representing the sacrifice and fear of the opposite sex to obtain the female's creative power. This legend sets the stage for patrilineal descent; monarchies have since passed from father to son.

Veneration for the Mother: Moon Goddesses

Veneration for the mother is found throughout Chinese history in the ideologies of Taoism and Buddhism, two religions that opposed Confucianism and fostered many protests to the social order in China. *The Book of Mountains and Sea* (from the Taoist religion) includes the story of Hsi Wang Mu, queen mother of the west, who lives in a palace on the mythical Jade Mountain in the west. She was originally a monster with a human face, tiger's teeth, and a leopard's tail; in Taoist legends, she became a beautiful goddess—female, embodying the principle of yin. A peach tree, which blooms only once every 3,000 years on the queen mother's birthday, grows there; those who eat its fruit gain immortality. It is at her birthday banquet that the legendary Monkey King stole a peach of immortality and was banished from heaven (Scott, 1980).

Chinese Buddhism, in turn, has the goddess Kuan Yin, whose cult equals and sometimes surpasses that of Buddha himself. Kuan Yin, the goddess of mercy, upon entering heaven is said to have paused to listen to the cry of the world. The derivation of this goddess comes from a story in 700 B.C. about the daughter of a ruler who refused to marry according to her parents' wishes; she was determined to enter a nunnery and devote her life to the poor and the sick (Scott, 1980). Buddhism and Taoism in Confucian China were often the refuge of women, since it acknowledged their equality with men, the contrasts between the peasants and nobility, and the contrasts between men and women.

In worship of gods and goddesses, the sun and moon have come to symbolize the essence of male and female, respectively. Many cultures believe the moon is a beneficent presence whose light is considered not only favorable, but also indispensable for growth. This contrasts to the sun's power that, in hot countries, seems hostile to life, scorching the earth and destroying living things. The moon is the fertilizing power, and therefore, often believed to cause pregnancy. The moon is changeable and cyclic, with its phases and its power to regenerate every month. Its essence, therefore, is female. For women, the life force ebbs and flows in their actual experiences, not only in nightly and daily rhythm as it does for men, but also in moon cycles and phases, producing a rhythm that waxes and wanes, ebbs and flows like the moon and ocean tides (Harding, 1971).

The moon goddess, with her fruit as the source for the drink of immortality, is unlike other goddesses; the moon mother has no male god who rules her. Instead, she is the mother of a son to be born again—that is, like Kuan Yin in the East or Virgin Mary in the West.

One Ch'ing dynasty (circa 18th-century) novel, *Flowers in the Mirror,* is both a fantasy and social satire on the plight of women. The author, believing in equal opportunity for men and women, sets the novel in the reign of Empress Wu, who usurped the throne from her son in the early T'ang dynasty (604–705 A.D.). As punishment for disobeying a decree, Tang Ao is dismissed from his scholarly rank and forsakes his world for a long journey in search of immortality. Not unlike the hero of *Gulliver's Travels,* he passes through many fantastic lands, where everything is strange, and comes to the Country of Women, where it is the women who are talented and pass the imperial examinations while the men stay at home.

Hua Muk Lan: The Woman Warrior

While these stories speak to the veneration of the mother and the fertilizing power of the moon goddess, they also reinforce the fears of women's power. This power is celebrated in the story of Hua Muk Lan, or the woman warrior as she is called in the West. One of the most celebrated classics in Chinese culture, Hua Muk Lan is the heroine of the Five Dynasties (420–588 A.D.). Her power lies in her ability to surpass the military skills of men. She is a young woman who loves and reveres her aging father so much that when he is called to battle, she goes in his place disguised as a man since he does not have a son. For 12 years she distinguishes herself in military battle as a warrior and leads the army to victory. She develops a friendship with a fellow military general whom she later marries after revealing her true self to him. She refuses further promotions, and instead returns home to her parents and family to fulfill her obligations to her family.

This Chinese classic contrasts with the theme of triangular conflict, which is celebrated in Western fairy tales such as Snow White and Cinderella, about the journey of an adolescent girl moving toward independence. There is a significant difference, however. In Asian stories, conflict is outside the home; the stories emphasize reunion between parent and child, and the absence of intergenerational conflict. The mother is the bystander, in contrast to Western fairy tales, where the father is the bystander. The developmental task of Hua Muk Lan is her replacement of her aging father—independence and separation—in contrast with Western fairy tales that emphasize the adolescent girl's beauty as competitive and threatening to the mother figure. The parents are not in conflict with the child's ascendance as they are in Western stories. Hua Muk Lan chooses to leave home to protect and rescue her father and to fulfill her responsibility and obligation to the family as the oldest sibling, a typical Chinese theme. It contrasts with the themes of sexual maturity favored in Western fairy tales, where the female is more passive and receptive. Snow White and Cinderella both need to overcome narcissism before they can unite with the prince.

Heroines of Strength and Power

The story of Hua Muk Lan persists in popularity among the Chinese who love her intelligence, cleverness, and responsibility to the family. Her journey, transformation, and military excellence or power can be achieved only if she ceases to live as a woman; she is celebrated particularly because this image is at odds with the subordinate roles of women during Confucian China (551–499 B.C.).

Despite society's veneration of the mother figure, most women were oppressed under Confucian and feudal society in China. A frequent theme in stories is that of the worthy Chinese woman, who braves death by letting herself be killed without flinching before the enemy, or by committing suicide, to facilitate the patriotic or revolutionary task of her husband or her clan. *The Guwen*, a collection of classical texts, illustrates this theme (Kristeva, 1986). The young heroine martyr, who commits suicide as a means of rebellion, is frequently celebrated in Chinese history. In communist China, women who committed themselves to ideals of emancipation often found no concrete means for realizing them other than through suicide; this was such a frequent occurrence that Mao Tse Tung wrote, "He who commits suicide is not motivated by a desire for death . . . it is most emphatic a demonstration of the will to live. The reason why people commit suicide in a society is that the society has seized their hopes and brutally crushed them" (quoted in Kristeva, 1986, p. 110).

In contemporary China, the bourgeois Revolution of 1912 and the May 4th Movement of 1919 were significant moments in the women's movement in China, because they threatened the Chinese family's patriarchy (Barlow & Bjorge, 1989; Kristeva, 1986). Despite the favoritism toward males during Confucian times and in communist China, there were women who transcended their roles to validate the strength of women. Ding Ling, one of China's most colorful and important women writers of the 20th century, was one such woman. Her writings in *I Myself Am a Woman* (Barlow & Bjorge, 1989) chart a feminist consciousness (from 1905–1985). She wrote about women and their emotion during a time when doing so was taboo. She also wrote of their plight and strivings to be seen as intellectual equals with men. She collided with the Communist Party, and was imprisoned by the Nationalists during the Cultural Revolution, well before the feminist movement in the West. Chinese women are often perceived by Westerners as being "behind Western women" in the women's movement when, in fact, the height of these intellectual and political movements in China occurred well before their zenith in America.

Chinese American immigrant women are the women warriors who have faced great odds and challenges in supporting families and culture as they coped with poverty, survival, male-dominated Confucian societies, and a racist America. This classic story has been rewritten in contemporary versions of *The Woman Warrior* (Kingston, 1989) and *Mulan,* an animated Disney film about Chinese American women.

MALE–FEMALE BONDS

The relationship between men and women is also captured in myths and symbols. Asian cultures describe and prescribe gender roles, as with the yin-yang balance of the universe; they cannot be independent of one another. Symbols of women merge the images of mother and wife, while those of men merge the images of father and son.

Sun Versus Moon Myths: Battle of the Sexes

The popular sun myth in Chinese culture is connected with the last of the five emperors, Yao, who was in danger of losing his throne. According to the story, there were ten suns that lived in the Valley of Light. At one point, all ten suns appeared in the sky at once and everything on earth was in danger of being burned. Emperor Yao gave a magic bow to Yi, the divine archer, who shot down nine of the suns, leaving only one. The sun is made of fire and symbolizes the male principle of yang. However, the divine archer had a wife, Ch'ang-O, who stole from him the herb of immortality, given to him by the queen mother of the west (Scott, 1980). As punishment, she was banished to the moon.

Women shine in the reflection of their husbands in this image, not unlike the relationship between the sun and the moon. In Confucian

Chinese literature, women were portrayed as seducers whose rise to power was often indirect or shameless. These stories about women often spoke of their beauty; their virtues included their unselfish loyalty and devotion to their husbands (Kristeva, 1986; Yu, 1974a, 1974b). These stories also combine history and legend to celebrate women of great character (i.e., clever and prowess) whose attempts to fulfill responsibilities involved significant conflict, sacrifice, and determination (Yu, 1974a, 1974b). In these stories, women tend to achieve their power as concubines or courtesans of the emperor, since this was typically their only access to positions of power during feudal times. One of these famous concubines frees herself from her role as servant to become empress, Wu Zetian. She accomplishes this by accusing the then-empress of killing her child, whom in fact she has killed herself. Her rule is characterized by her independent and even fearsome lifestyle. Her Buddhist origins support the equality of the sexes; she uses her newfound power to undercut the influence of the ruling class in this Confucian society and institutes the system of competitive examinations for civil servants.

Mother–Son Bonds

Male–female relationships in Asian culture are also portrayed in stories about mother–son bonds. While the journey of separation-individuation or independence from parents is a major theme, the importance of a son's loyalty and obligation to the family is also stressed. Many Chinese myths and stories emphasize the importance of the bond between mother and son, while Western stories emphasize the triangular conflict of a couple against an interfering mother-in-law. The figure of the mother in Chinese stories is often benevolent and supportive.

Several classic Chinese stories speak of a mother's influence on her son, and are frequently recited by mothers to their children. While the father of Confucius is generally unknown, his mother plays an important role as his protector and inspiration. Yueh Fei was a famous patriot and military leader of the Sung dynasty. His mother, Yau, is famous because the Chinese believe his bravery and loyalty to China came from his mother's lessons and the four words she tattooed on his back: "Be patriotic to the country." The development of Mencius, another famous Chinese philosopher, was attributed largely to the influence of his mother, who moved three times to ensure that they lived in an environment conducive to development of his character, moving the last time next to a school where he imitated the scholars. These stories were adapted in the contemporary Asian American novel *The Woman Warrior* (Kingston, 1989).

Oedipus and Ajase Complex: Triangular Conflict

In Western culture and literature, the Oedipus complex, which emphasizes male development and the father–son bond, stands in stark contrast to the Ajase complex within Asian culture, which emphasizes the mother–son bond. The contrasts between these two myths define cultural differences between the East and the West, although there are common universal themes. Similarly, in both tales, the unlikely hero, the boy or the son, proves himself through slaying dragons, solving riddles, and living by his wits and goodness.

Here is the story of Oedipus: Terrified by the prophecy that his child would murder his father and marry his mother, Laius, the king of Thebes, withdraws from his wife. In order to conceive a son, she gets him drunk and seduces him. Laius pierces the baby boy's feet and leaves him to die. The baby is rescued by a shepherd who names the child Oedipus, meaning swollen foot. He is presented to King Polybus and later becomes heir. In seeking advice about who his parents are, he is told of the oracle. Shocked, he leaves their court.

On the road out of the city, he encounters King Laius, his biological father. In the confrontation as to who should pass first, Oedipus kills his father. He meets up with the Sphinx, who terrorizes Thebans by refusing passage to those who cannot answer its riddles. Oedipus answers the riddle, thereby freeing the Thebans of their domination. Oedipus becomes king and unknowingly marries Jocasta, his mother. A plague falls on Thebes because this violation of the basic laws of gods could not go unpunished. In trying to rid Thebes of the plague, Oedipus finds out his true origins. Queen Jocasta hangs herself. Oedipus, seized with remorse and disgust, gouges out his own eyes, and takes to wandering the earth.

In contrast to the "Oedipus complex," where a boy has murderous wishes against his father and erotic desires for his mother, the Asian Ajase complex, based on an Indian myth, emphasizes the intensity of the mother–son relationship. Prince Ajase, who was destined to kill his father, becomes king, as does Oedipus. He later tries to kill his mother because she is loyal to his father, the dead king. However, Ajase feels too guilty and cannot accomplish this. As punishment for his transgressions, sores develop on his body and an odor emanates from them that is so offensive, no one will come near. His mother is the only person willing to care for him. King Ajase's heart responds to his mother's display of affection and forgiveness; thus, he and his mother are reunited (Okonogi, quoted by Tatara, 1980, in Chin et al., 1993).

Balance of Power Between the Sexes: Male Dominance

As these myths of mother–son and husband–wife bonds suggest, the mother or wife takes an active role in both Asian and Western mythology. As wife, in both Asian and Western mythology, woman is the temptress whose rise to power is shameless. As mother in Asian mythology, she is powerful, benevolent, forgiving, nurturing, and a mentor. This contrasts with Western mythology, where she is either weak or wicked.

As we translate these stories into the lives of Chinese American immigrant families, the celebration of female strengths is subordinated to male dominance in both American and Chinese societies. Female strengths remained covert, because their implied threat to male power was destructive.

FAMILY AND GENERATIONAL BONDS

The family unit is of great significance in Chinese culture, and is defined to include the extended family. While family is important in most cultures, the emphasis on loyalty and obligation to the family in Chinese culture is unparalleled, with its origins in Confucianism.

Confucianism and Taoism

Prior to the establishment of the Republic of China, Chinese families followed the Confucian tradition, which prescribed a hierarchical order of relationships stressing the importance of filial piety and ancestor worship. It is these characteristics that are most commonly known in the West as "Chinese culture." In an agrarian society, the passage of land from father to son and the need for physical labor was essential to the survival of the family. The family was essentially an economic unit in which males were dominant. Confucianism ensured this continuity by stressing the son's reverence for his father and his role as the heir apparent to the ancestral line.

Submissiveness to authority of the family and government was emphasized. Women and children were subordinate to men. Males were esteemed and valued. They were allowed to have multiple wives as a demonstration of their wealth and social status. The only true mother was the first wife; all others were considered concubines, who were of greater value if they produced sons. In order to enhance the power of the family, the children of all the wives belonged to the first wife or Dai Ma (Eldest Mother). The power in the family rested with the father, eldest son, and grandmother or eldest mother (Kristeva, 1986).

Familiarity between father and daughter was more permissible, different from the distance, formality, and severity that was expected between father and son. While this gave women more latitude in their behavior, it also meant a total disregard of females in a social order where males reigned as the ancestors to be worshipped. Under Confucianism, women were destined only for housework and reproduction. The words of several Confucian scholars suggest the need to suppress the strivings of women. Yang Chen of the Han dynasty said, "If women are given work that requires contact with the outside, they will sow disorder and confusion throughout the Empire" (Kristeva, 1986, p. 76). Sima Guang of the Song dynasty said, "Give a woman an education and all you will get from her is boredom and complaints" (Kristeva, 1986, p. 76).

Confucianism pervaded Chinese American society during the early wave Toisanese immigrants to the United States; most Chinese immigrants were well versed in classic Confucian teachings transmitted through storytelling or reading of the classics, and behaved in accordance with its principles. Most important were the principles of filial piety illustrated by the *Twenty-Four Stories of Filial Piety* (see Tseng & Hsu, 1972); these classic stories prescribed moral principles for the relationship between generations, extolling the virtues of industriousness, respect for one's parents, and obligation to the family. They have been influential in Chinese childrearing, analogous to books by Dr. Benjamin Spock.

The Taoist and Buddhist religions, on the other hand, never ceased to fight the Confucian paternalistic hierarchy. Women in China embraced Taoism as a religion because it emphasized the equality of women and men. Westerners often fail to realize this ambivalence within the Chinese psyche, and the parallel challenge to Confucianism.

Triumph of the Elders: Intergenerational

In Chinese folklore and stories of the Confucian tradition, defiance of parental authority results in the admonition, punishment, or death of the transgressor (i.e., the children). If children survive these transgressions in folklore, they are given the opportunity for training and atonement. In conflicts between generations, the elders always triumph (Tseng & Hsu, 1972). Many of the *Twenty-Four Stories of Filial Piety* deal with how the son obtains food for his mother. In five of these stories, the mother is sick and special food is required for her recovery. The stories also emphasize that it is ideal for families to maintain continuity without conflict between generations. The parent is expected to protect the child, and the child in turn is expected to return this kindness in adulthood, which shows mutual dependence between generations.

The powerfulness of parental authority is presented in another classic Chinese story of a young couple in love against the wishes of their parents; they are unsuccessful in their defiance and are united only upon their death when they transform into a pair of butterflies.

These stories contrast with Western fairy tales such as Hansel and Gretel, whose parents are poor and worry about how to take care of their children. In this tale, the children decide to leave home together because they fear that their parents are plotting to desert them and starve them to death. The experience of mother abandonment is paramount here, which is opposed to the Asian theme of maternal protection and benevolence. Their journey takes them to the gingerbread house of the witch or bad mother. The witch's evil design forces the children to recognize the dangers of unrestrained oral greed and dependence. In relying on ego and intelligent assessment, they are able to trick the witch into climbing into the oven, thereby freeing them (Bettelheim, 1976).

THE JOURNEY: TRANSFORMATION

As we journey through life, we seek to reach a state of enlightenment. Immigrant families similarly make their journey in a quest for freedom and enlightenment. While the Garden of Eden lies in the East for Americans, the Jade Mountain of the queen mother, Hsi Wang Mu, lies in the West for Asians. According to both Western and Asian mythology, those who seek enlightenment need only travel there to eat its fruit. In both traditions, there is but one forbidden fruit: the apple in the Garden of Eden, and the peach from the Jade Mountain—the former for those seeking knowledge, the latter for those seeking immortality. The eating of either fruit has wrought havoc on those who disobey. However, the images of women differ in Eastern and Western mythology. The balance of power shifts. It is Eve who tempts Adam to eat the forbidden apple (i.e., the woman tempts the man), while it is

Monkey King who steals the immortal peach from the queen mother (i.e., the son steals from the mother).

Interdependence

The developmental task of achieving adulthood is portrayed in many stories of sisterhood and brotherhood; these are stories of self-actualization, identity, transformation, and enlightenment. In *Grimm's Fairy Tales* of Western culture, brother and sister themes often feature the adventures of two siblings representing disparate natures of the self, which must be integrated for human happiness. Transformations to an animal existence represent impulse and instinctual desires, while reversion back to human form denotes achieving maturity. This transformation usually requires a journey and leaving the orbit of the home. One such Grimm fairy tale, "Brother and Sister," begins with a lack of differentiation between two siblings, whose wanderings lead them to a spring. Brother gives in to his instinctual desires, and after drinking from the spring, he turns into a fawn. Sister vows never to leave her brother and protects him until he returns to his human form. Both go through transformations before achieving maturity (Bettelheim, 1976).

Chinese literature often emphasizes the importance of interdependence and teamwork in the journey to enlightenment, as in the tale of "Seven Brothers." This is a fairy tale of seven loyal brothers who set out to please their father. The emperor set a heavy tax on the brothers' lucrative land. The brothers embark on a journey to reason with the emperor to protect their land and their father. They meet with resistance, and it is only by teaming together with their different supernatural assets that they are able to overcome the emperor: "Together we stand invincible" (Chang, 1968, p. 64).

Romance of the Three Kingdoms: Chivalry and Obligation

Romance of the Three Kingdoms is one of the great Chinese classics, a literary masterpiece written by Luo Guanzhong in the 13th century. It begins during the Ming Dynasty and ends in the founding of the Chin Dynasty (265–420 A.D.) during the golden age of chivalry in Chinese history. The semifictional novel includes tales of military exploit as brothers contest for the throne and kingdoms are conquered.

After the last of the Han emperors was assassinated, China was divided into three feudal kingdoms. The end of the Han dynasty was one of the most turbulent periods in China's history, when corruption was rampant in the imperial court. Coupled with natural disasters such as floods, plague, and locust swarms, widespread hunger and dissatisfaction among the peasants escalated until the Yellow Scarves Rebellion, led by Zhang Jiao, broke out (so named because the rebels tied yellow scarves on their heads). Unable to put down the rebellion with government troops, Emperor Ling issued a call to warlords across the country for assistance in suppressing the rebellion. This resulted in a struggle for power among the warlords, rendering the Han emperor powerless.

Out of this struggle in the early 220s A.D. emerged the sovereignty of three smaller states: Wei, Wu, and Shu. Historians debate over which of these three kingdoms was the legitimate heir to the Han dynasty, although they now generally recognize the Wei Kingdom created by Cao Cao as the official imperial line or Mandate of Heaven (see http://www.3kingdoms.net/intro.htm).

The tales of courage and adventure in this classic literary masterpiece of more than 1,700 years ago are still popular among the Chinese today; the heroes—Liu Bei, Cao Cao, Kuan Yu, Zhang Fei, and Zhuge Liang—are household names. *Romance of the Three Kingdoms* is not only about the struggle and conflicts among the warlords; it is about loyalty, betrayal, courage, lust, determination, responsibilities, repaying the kindness of others, and trust among brothers; it is about chivalry and obligation to serve one's country within the Chinese culture.

The stories are used as examples of brotherhood, loyalty, and obligation as three brothers fight for the throne—values that guide behavior in Chinese American immigrant families. The mother–son bond between Liu Bei and his mother is reiterated as a virtue. Male aggression is celebrated through the cunning of military strategy and adventures of the military campaigns; the transformation of the hero is in his leadership and reinforces Confucian values and principles. There is much symbolism in the animal names of the generals, whose characteristics reflect their leadership styles. The peach orchard in which the oath among the brothers was sworn is the symbol of immortality.

Books have been written about Chinese military strategy from this period, and are used to understand characteristics of modern leadership. The heroes of this classic are often studied for their character traits and how they contribute to effective leadership styles. Thus, this classical novel remains popular because it illustrates the journey taken by its heroes, and provides insight into human character and the human condition within Chinese culture. It is comparable to discussing the impact of the Revolutionary War in America.

Journey to the West Versus *Star Wars*: Transformation

Journey to the West and *Star Wars* are two sagas that illustrate some differences between Asian and Western culture, respectively. Although they are stories of adventure, underlying themes speak to transformation of character and the achievement of enlightenment. *Journey to the West,* a renowned 16th-century epic written by Wu Ch'eng, is an allegorical rendition of a journey in search of the scriptures; it is mingled with Chinese fables, fairy tales, legends, and demon adventures with origins in the Taoist and Buddhist religions. It is based on the true story of a famous Chinese monk, Xuan Zang (602–664 A.D.), who lived in the 5th century A.D. After years of traveling on foot to what is now India, the birthplace of Buddhism, to seek the Sutra, the Buddhist holy book, he goes through many trials and tribulations. After returning to China with the *sutras*—or to Tang Mountain (Tang San) as China was called at that time—his translation of them into Chinese contributes greatly to the development of Buddhism in China.

Journey to the West is divided into three parts: (1) an early history of the Monkey spirit; (2) a pseudo-historical account of Hsuan-Tsang's family and life before his trip to the western heaven; and (3) the main story, consisting of 81 dangers and calamities encountered by Hsuan-Tsang and his three animal spirit disciples.

Three disciples join Hsuan-Tsang on his quest—the clever and impudent Monkey, the gluttonous Pig, and the river spirit, Sha Monk; representing mind, body, and spirit, respectively. The team travels for 16 years, encountering adventures with supernatural and mythic beings, and fighting fearsome battles with demons and spirits, all the while guided by the compassionate goddess Kuan Yin. The external adventures are colorful, action oriented, and full of fantasy; the four travelers need to learn to distinguish truth from fiction and demons from spirits, and avoid being fooled by appearances. These external adventures are paralleled by inward explorations of the human psyche within each of the characters, who become enlightened and achieve a transformation in the process of this journey.

Journey to the West is not unlike the popular Western epic *Star Wars,* termed a "modern developmental fairy tale" by McDermott and Lum (1980). *Star Wars* takes place in another galaxy in the distant past. It is a trilogy of adventure that center around three characters—Luke Skywalker, Han Solo, and Princess Leia—who are forced to band together by circumstance rather than friendship. At the beginning, Princess Leia, a leader of the Rebel Alliance, is captured and taken aboard the evil Galactic Empire's mobile command station, the impregnable Death Star. Prior to her capture, she entrusts the plans to destroy the Death Star to R2D2, the little robot, hoping he and his caretaker, C3PO, also a robot, can reach a former general of the Old Republic, Obi-Wan Kenobi. The robots end up becoming farm hands for the uncle of Luke Skywalker. After Luke's uncle and aunt are killed, the three embark on their adventure to save the planet. They engage Han Solo, a mercenary pilot, to rescue Princess Leia. Despite great odds and many adventures, the trio, with the help of "the Force" is able to destroy the Death Star. This saga has many things in common with *Journey to the West:* the elements of fantasy, supernatural powers, good versus evil, and action. The trio also goes through a transformation and travels under the support of the Force.

There are significant contrasts between the two sagas that distinguish their cultural origins. In *Journey to the West,* the parents are symbolically represented by female authority figures—the spiritual and supreme beings of Kuan Yin and Hsi Wang Mu, who watch over the travelers. In *Star Wars,* the parent is represented by male authority figure Obi-Wan Kenobi, who watches over the trio, and by Darth Vader, another male authority figure, who thwarts, threatens, and almost destroys the trio. These two represent two opposing sides of a powerful force. The need to destroy the parental authority figures in Western mythology as the hero goes through his transformation and maturation is what distinguishes it from Asian mythology, where the benevolent authority figure remains intact.

Both Monkey King and Luke Skywalker long for adventure and are impatient; their transformation is analogous to adolescent maturation. In *Journey to the West,* components of self are embodied in the characters of Monkey, Pig, and River Spirit—that is, impulse, bodily desire, and spirit; the developmental task is in their moderation and containment. In *Star Wars,* Luke's idealism is pitted against Han Solo's cynicism, selfishness, and sense of omnipotence; the developmental task is in his self-expression.

Repressed images of childhood are depicted in both sagas. The barroom (cantina) in *Star Wars* is like a frontier saloon and embodies visual evidence of evil and ugliness, representing the present corrupt world. In *Journey to the West,* the seduction by the material world is represented in the substory of Seven Spider Spirits. The Tang priest is lured into Gossamer Cave by seven spider spirits disguised as beautiful women. His rescue by Monkey and Pig emphasize the importance of interdependence and teamwork.

The fight between good and evil is a spiritual one in the story of Monkey King. Monkey King fights demon spirits while Luke Skywalker fights the evil Empire. In *Star Wars*, the ultimate fight is between father and son as Luke Skywalker discovers that the Darth Vader of the evil Empire is his father. The journey to adulthood is played out differently once again; the son must be victorious over the powerful father figure in Western literature. By contrast, the emphasis in Asian literature is in the transformation of Monkey King with the result that he is granted forgiveness and immortality by the queen mother, Hsi Wang Mu.

The journey for each is also different. Han Solo and Luke Skywalker are out to destroy the evil forces; they succeed because the vulnerability of the Death Star was in its designer's inability to conceive of the fact that one small spaceship could be a threat to it—symbolizing the failing of the father to see the threat of the son. By contrast, Monkey King makes a journey to seek the scriptures—for enlightenment, as opposed to conquering. Luke must conquer and overcome Darth Vader to achieve his maturity and manhood, whereas Monkey King must subdue his impulsive and temperamental tendencies to achieve enlightenment, represented by the crown, which gives him headaches whenever he has bad thoughts. The rebelliousness and cunning of Monkey King is internal and must be contained in order to succeed over the demons and spirits outside.

These differences reflect different worldviews of man against nature. In Asian culture, man must establish harmony with nature, while in Western culture man must overcome it. Both epics are appealing because they tap into the meaning of life; self-identity and value systems; separation and individuation; achievement of maturity; and overcoming of problems of dependency, abandonment, and death.

JOURNEY TO THE WEST: IMMIGRATION

Journey to the West is an allegory for the journey of immigration. Many also agree that the hero, Monkey King, who is full of cunning, prowess, and wisdom, is also an allegory for a rebellious spirit against the then-untouchable feudal rulers in China. His plight is not unlike the trials and challenges that all Chinese American immigrants must face before achieving enlightenment. Monkey King is punished for hundreds of years, but remains rebellious and formidable against his parental figures. His transformation is not unlike that of Chinese American immigrants in creating their bicultural identity.

Monkey King: Cunning and Rebellious

An examination of the beloved character Monkey King in Chinese folklore is important to capture the psyche and transformation process of Chinese American immigrants (see http://www.china-on-site.com/pages/comic/comiccatalog1.php). Monkey King is a rebellious and extraordinary being, born out of a rock, fertilized by the grace of heaven. Being extremely smart and cunning, he learned all the magic tricks and kung fu from a master Taoist; he is able to transform himself into 72 different images, such as a tree, bird, beast of prey, or bug as small as a mosquito to sneak into an enemy's belly and fight him from the inside.

Using clouds as a vehicle, he can travel 180,000 *li* (miles) in a single somersault; he carries a huge iron bar that can expand or shrink at his command as his favorite weapon in his feats. He claims to be king in defiance of the authority and Supreme Being—the Great Jade Emperor. That act of treason, coupled with complaints from the masters of the four seas and hell invites the relentless scourge of the heavenly army. After many showdowns, the emperor, unable to defeat him, has to offer the monkey an official title to appease him. Enraged when he learns that the position he held was nothing but that of a stable keeper, he revolts, fighting his way back to earth to resume his own claim as king.

Eventually, the heavenly army subdues him after many battles with the help of all the god warriors. Because he has a bronze head and iron shoulders, all methods of execution fail and Monkey King dulls many a sword inflicted upon him. As a last resort, the emperor commands that he be burned in the furnace where his Taoist minister, Tai Shang Lao Jun, refines his pills of immortality. Instead of killing him, the fire and smoke adds to Monkey King a pair of fiery golden crystal eyes that can see through what people normally cannot. He fights his way down again. Finally, with Buddha's help, Monkey King is suppressed under a great mountain known as the Mount of Five Fingers and he could not move. Five hundred years later, he is rescued by the Tang priest Hsuan Tsang, and becomes his disciple on the journey to the west.

Eighty-One Trials to Enlightenment

In *Journey to the West,* the goddesses and parental authority put the Tang priest and his three disciples through 81 tests before they can obtain the scriptures and reach enlightenment. The number 81 is a multiple of nine times nine, with the number nine symbolizing longevity or immortality; the struggle is transcendence to another level of consciousness, or heaven in Western terms. As Monkey King so aptly puts it, he can leap a thousand *li* (i.e., miles) to get to where he wants to in a second, but he must accompany the Tang priest on foot to reach his destiny in 16 years; the developmental process cannot be rushed. Similarly the number sixteen is a multiple of four times four with the number four symbolizing death.

Journey of Immigration

The early Toisanese Chinese immigrants were known for their rebellious seafaring spirit. Their suffering, rendered by the floods wreaking havoc on the crops and causing massive starvation, forced the immigration in search of the Golden Mountain of the West (i.e., the San Francisco gold rush). During their journey, they faced major trials and tribulations, including having to fight with the racist policies of anti-Asian sentiment and legislation. The fight against the heavenly army is not unlike the immigration experience. The journey to the west is the journey made by immigrants to the golden mountains in San Francisco.

The character of Monkey King is not unlike the unbreakable spirit of Chinese American immigrants. Early Toisanese immigrants were described as cunning and devious for their tendency to be "inscrutable." These negative portrayals and stereotypes are not unlike the cunning and rebelliousness of Monkey King, who is loved by the Chinese as a smart and spirited character. Monkey King's rebelliousness against feudal rulers of China is similar to the rebelliousness of Chinese immigrants against the unjust and racist policies of the United States. Many immigrants defied the rules that they consider senseless and unjust during the years of illegal immigration as they sought to survive and reunite with families in the United States.

CHAPTER 2

Contemporary Storytelling and Immigration Legend

In Search Of

In our lifetime, we allow destiny to pass us by,
It's unpredictable but there's no telling why.
Through its low tides and ripping waves,
we manage to survive.
Our strength gives us the chance
to get over the troubled waters alive.

Opening up to new beginnings is a way to rediscover. . . .
The confusions amongst our inner selves
that we may try to cover.
Over the mountains, we will climb to the top,
Searching for new heights that we can adopt.

Tracey Lynette Ong

THE CREATION OF LEGEND: WARRIOR IMAGES

Storytelling continues in contemporary times. Those that capture our imagination and provide answers to us about the cycle of life create new legends and myths. *Star Wars* (Lucas, 1977), *Crouching Tiger, Hidden Dragon* (Lee, 2004), and *The Woman Warrior* (Kingston, 1989) are several such stories that feature women in warrior roles. Cast in contemporary and futuristic contexts, the stories continue to draw on cultural images, themes, and values of the past while modified by our global contexts involving journey and adventure.

Crouching Tiger, Hidden Dragon: Identity Transformation

Ang Lee's movie *Crouching Tiger, Hidden Dragon* is a contemporary film set in the 19th century that creates legend and myth based on Chinese culture. Its popularity and impact lies in how it impresses the power of myth upon those of us who thought it was lost (Simpson, 2001). Unlike classic Asian myths, the main protagonists are female. Yet like many Asian classics, it concludes with the death or suicide of the main protagonists, the lovers' union ending in tragedy, and the benevolence of the symbolic mother.

According to Campbell (1949), several characters in myths are constants: hero, mentor, shadow, and trickster. The hero's journey typically results in his or her transformation—the eternal struggle for identity, in Western myths, or enlightenment, in Eastern myths. Such stories are appealing because we are each on a similar journey in real life. Adapting a 1930s Chinese novel by Wang Du Lu, Ang Lee crafted a "dream of China" where the everyday merges with the fantastical by using a format common in Chinese martial arts movies. However, *Crouching Tiger, Hidden Dragon* is different from the classical hero's journey, which typically involves a male rite of passage; in this movie, Ang Lee creates a feminine tale of self-discovery. Therefore, it is both classic and feminist.

Shu Lien, the heroine, arrives in Beijing and observes two young girls entertaining on the street. She is disdainful because she views these girls as slaves; yet she too is trapped by her fate to remain a warrior. She envies the "freedom" of the princess Jen to be the feminine Asian female.

In the movie, the ancient sword of legendary warrior Li Mu Bai (the male mentor) is stolen. In seeking enlightenment, he gave up his sword and entrusted it to his female warrior ally, Shu Lien, to take to Governor Yu in Beijing for safekeeping. The sword is stolen by the trickster princess Jen, and protected by Jade Fox, the shadowy nemesis who killed Li Mu Bai's mentor. Li Mu Bai is forced to become a warrior again in order to avenge his mentor's death.

Both Li Mu Bai and Jade Fox want Jen as their disciple, but are deceived by her—an intergenerational theme. Li Mu Bai and Shu Lien represent the good parental figures who remain true to their virtues and character, clearly an Asian theme; both suppress their feelings toward one another during their many years together as warrior allies. Shu Lien does not marry or fulfill her love for Li Mu Bai out of loyalty to his brother, to whom she was engaged—an Asian female virtue but a bondage of culture values.

Li Mu Bai embodies the characteristics of both the "crouching tiger" and the "hidden dragon." He demonstrates his military prowess in his masterful use of martial arts—a characteristic of the tiger. When he comes in touch with his affectionate feelings for Shu Lien, he plans to give up the sword in his quest for enlightenment—a characteristic of the dragon. In Western culture, this quest is an embodiment of his "feminine side" or emotional side, while in Asian culture, it is a juxtaposition of his male and female characteristics (Simpson, 2001).

The spectacular martial arts feats are legendary in Chinese classics. Green Destiny, Li Mu Bai's sword, has obvious parallels to the Western legendary sword Excalibur of King Arthur. The rooftop chase between Jen and Li Mu Bai mirrors those of the classic *Arabian Nights*.

The flashback encounter between the young lovers, Jen and Lo (she is the dragon and he is the tiger) in the Gobi Desert is free and impulsive, in contrast with that of the older lovers, which is contained and suppressed. Jen is an upstart aristocrat who goes through various transformations of spoiled brat, errant thief, hearty fighter, and passionate lover. She is the trickster and heroine, her admirable qualities conflicting with her darker side and impulses. The full extent of her powers is revealed in the bar fight. Li Mu Bai wants to be her mentor, believing that her purer qualities will prevail. She makes a formidable opponent and while both Li Mu Bai and Shu Lien end up in combat with Jen, neither have the heart to kill her.

Symbolism and Character Development

Crouching Tiger, Hidden Dragon taps deeply into ancient Chinese myths. Criticisms cited by Simpson about the movie as being "nothing more than a bag of tricks" reflect a failure of many Westerners to understand the symbolism and values of Asian culture. Angered at Jen's betrayal (she steals the martial arts secrets by exploiting Jade Fox's inability to read the stolen book), Jade Fox attempts to poison Jen. In attempting to rescue her, Li Mu Bai is poisoned by Jade Fox. Jen is too late in her attempts to find an antidote. The movie ends with Jen, the young female protagonist, taking a "leap of faith" as a reward for becoming a "pure warrior"; the ending is ambiguous as to whether this is a suicide (a common ending in Asian classics) to atone for her guilt and responsibility for Li Mu Bai's death.

Crouching Tiger, Hidden Dragon is a movie rich in symbolism. The dragon in Chinese mythology is a beneficent figure, blessed, and chief of all the reptiles with powers of transformation—Li Mu Bai's transformation is internal; Jen's is external. In Christian mythology, by contrast, the dragon is a symbol of sin and evil. It is often represented as crushed under the feet of saints and martyrs, symbolizing the triumph of Christianity over paganism. The Chinese dragon symbolizes power and excellence, valiancy and boldness, heroism and perseverance, nobility and divinity. A dragon overcomes obstacles until success is his. He is energetic, decisive, optimistic, intelligent, and ambitious. The dragon confers the essence of life in the form of its sheng chi (celestial breath) and bestows its power in the form of the seasons, bringing water from rain, warmth from the sunshine, wind from the seas, and soil from the earth. The dragon is the ultimate representation of the forces of mother nature, the greatest divine force on earth.

These dragon characteristics of Jen are hidden when she is behaving as the aristocratic princess, which is shown by her impatience to reveal her hidden power and other self. This story is both atypical and contemporary in its portrayal of male and female characteristics, given that it features women warriors with dragon characteristics. The identity struggle in this story is contemporary because the main protagonists search for enlightenment in a journey that mirrors the transformation process of Chinese American immigrants.

THE WOMAN WARRIOR: CHINESE AMERICAN PARADOX

The Woman Warrior: Memoirs of a Girlhood Among Ghosts, by Maxine Hong Kingston (1989), is a contemporary novel of an American-born daughter of Chinese immigrant parents. It illustrates the paradoxical nature of the Chinese American experience through the eyes of an American-born Chinese using family history, "talk-story," memory, legend, and imaginative projection. Speaking from two vantage points, the narrator sees double almost all of the time. Secrets are never said in front of the *bak gwai* (white demons); culture is lived and not explained. These practices are confusing and nonsensical unless understood within a cultural context. Although the novel alludes to the many nuances characteristic of Chinese American immigrant families, critics have challenged the author's distortion of Chinese legends. Kingston argues that it is not a chronicle of history, but a novel, and records the legends as it is remembered.

One of the most critical contradictions facing the Chinese American woman (i.e., the character) in *The Woman Warrior* is the relationship between her perceptions of her Chinese heritage and American realities. For the Chinese American girl, the maddening paradox is that the same culture that produced the No-Name Woman—that is, the aunt who drowned herself in the family well—and Moon Orchid (the aunt who ends up insane) also produced Fa Mu Lan (the woman warrior) and Brave Orchid, the mother who defies all images of the subservient, passive Chinese American female. Like Fa Mu Lan, the sword of the Chinese American female avenger is used to avenge; vengeance is not with beheading, but with words. The Chinese American woman warrior must respond to the continual throat pain that returns unless she speaks what she thinks is the truth, to report crimes and to "talk-story" herself. Because the American-born Chinese woman must confront dualities and contradictions, she is blessed with a special gift: "I learned to make my mind large, as the universe is large so that there is room for paradoxes" (p. 29). *The Woman Warrior* is about a Chinese American woman's attempt to find her voice and fight the contradictions of Chinese and American culture. The novel is a celebration of strength and rejection of sentimentality and self-pity (E.H. Kim, 1981). The names of the characters in the novel are symbolic of the tension and struggle of Chinese immigrant women.

MOTHER–DAUGHTER BONDS: FAMILY SAGA

Stories of mother–daughter bonds are more abundant in contemporary literature, coinciding with the women's movement. The connection among women in their relationships is celebrated. Classic Chinese stories tend to emphasize the closeness of the mother–son relationship together with themes of family obligation and loyalty.

Western Fairy Tales: Triumph of the Daughter

Classic Western fairy tales typically portray the mother as the villain, and the mother–daughter relationship as competitive, where the daughter replaces or is triumphant over the mother figure. Snow White, for example, is about an adolescent girl beset by a jealous stepmother, the queen, who tries to destroy her because she is more beautiful. When the queen issues an order to kill her, the servants instead abandon her in the forest, thus saving her life. When the queen again tries to destroy her, the dwarfs rescue her. She finally succumbs to a deathlike sleep after tempted with a poisoned apple from the stepmother. A handsome prince falls in love with her beauty and rescues her. During the journey, the poisoned apple is jarred loose and Snow White regains consciousness. The queen dies (from jealousy), and the couple live happily ever after.

Cinderella, another favorite Western fairy tale, is about a beautiful, patient, and modest adolescent girl who is forced to perform menial tasks and is rejected by her two spoiled, haughty, and heartless stepsisters. After Cinderella's mother dies, her father marries a cruel stepmother who is jealous of her beauty as an emerging adolescent. Unbeknownst to her stepmother and stepsisters, Cinderella attends the 3-day celebration as a princess, during which the prince becomes enthralled with her. In her haste to leave the ball before midnight to avoid being transformed back to her original self in rags, she loses her glass slipper. The prince sets out to find his true love and the rightful owner of this slipper.

Like many Western fairy tales, there is competition and heightened rivalry between mother and daughter over who is more beautiful. The 3 days symbolize three stages of maturation or developmental tasks that Cinderella must go through before she can achieve the maturity and integration of self to meet her prince face-to-face. The mother figure is typically split. In the story of Snow White, the good pre-Oedipal mother—that is, the all-giving, all protecting mother—dies early in the story while the bad Oedipal mother (i.e., the depriving, selfish, rejecting, and unjust mother), represented by the jealous queen, tries to deny the heroine an independent existence. The father is mostly absent and unable to rescue or to protect Snow White, for she must journey on her own (Heuscher, 1974). These fairy tales portray females in passive and receptive roles with characters of innocence and beauty; they are victim to the external forces besetting them in a journey of sexual maturation, and of separation and independence; they need to be rescued by a charming prince.

The Joy Luck Club: Bonds and Bondage

The Joy Luck Club (Tan, 1989), a contemporary novel by Amy Tan, is about the lives of four Chinese American immigrant women and their daughters. The portraits of the intergenerational relationships illustrate the influence of culture and immigration on the psychological adjustment of the characters. They are slaves to their past, a fact that both bonds them together and puts them in bondage. Historical Chinese culture and themes in this contemporary novel celebrate women as nurturing mothers and capture the struggles, developmental crises, and character transformations of these women in evolving a bicultural identity. Two of the mother–daughter relationships are chosen for analysis here because they represent the rescue fantasy and warrior image of women, so characteristic in the fairy tales and myths being discussed.

The character of An-Mei Hsu portrays the rescue fantasy, the bondage of fate, and how the theme of separation and abandonment is recurrent through several generations in her family. Born of the element water[1] (symbolic of women), she is raised by her grandmother because her mother brought shame to the family. According to family lore, her mother ran off to marry a rich man after her husband died. An-Mei later discovers that her mother was actually raped as a ruse to dishonor her and force her to marry this man in order to bear him a son. Her mother returns to the dying grandmother; she cuts a piece of her flesh to be boiled in a medicinal soup, symbolic of the highest sacrifice of a daughter to her mother in a consciously fruitless attempt to heal. The boiling water scars An-Mei as she rushes to join her mother against her grandmother's wishes. She almost dies of suffocation, and it is only the grandmother's threat of abandonment that brings her back. An-Mei's mother later commits suicide (i.e., once again abandoning her) as the only way she knows to guarantee An-Mei's safe status in her husband's household; her husband was forced to honor An-Mei forever or run the risk of retribution and wrath from her mother's spirit. In doing so, she achieved for her daughter through her death what she could not do in her life.

A motto in Chinese society is that it is better to die with honor than to live with shame. During Confucian society, a woman's sanctity and honor belonged to her husband; rape marked the defilement of women's honor. During an era when women were without choices, it was not uncommon for women to choose suicide as a means of regaining their honor.

The myth in An-Mei's family is that "an ancestor once stole water from a sacred well, and now water steals her son away." This is An-Mei's explanation when her daughter's inattention results in her son being drowned at sea on a family outing. (It also symbolizes the family curse, because her mother's rape brought shame to the family; she is then rejected, in the tradition of blaming women as sexual seducers while forgiving men for their impulsiveness and carnal desires.) An-Mei brings out the family Bible in a consciously fruitless attempt to bring her son back; she cries in despair for being so foolish to think she could use faith to change fate.

An-Mei rescues her daughter from her marriage to a white dermatologist. Her daughter, Rose, spends 17 years in a dependent and unhealthy marriage whereby her husband constantly rescues her emotionally. In despair over her failing marriage and impending divorce, Rose attempts suicide. As An-Mei helps her daughter heal from her psychological pain, she is able to resolve her own issues of separation and abandonment. Mother and daughter plant a seedling together, nourished by water, symbolic of their new start. Rose is able to move from dependency to a healthy interdependence with her mother.

The character of Lindo Jong in *The Joy Luck Club* offers a somewhat different portrayal of Chinese American women, more similar to the classic Chinese story of Hua Mu Lan, the Woman Warrior. Worried that her grandchildren will forget her, Lindo's mother gives her a gold bracelet, symbolic of the purity and genuineness of Chinese culture and character. Born without metal[2] but of good character, Lindo comes from a poor upbringing, and is married into a well-to-do family at age 16 when her family is forced to leave (i.e., abandoning her) because of the floods. The marriage is loveless and is not consummated. Unable to produce an heir, Lindo is blamed by her mother-in-law for being too balanced with the metal—meaning the gold, which she brought with her to the marriage.

Given that divorce was taboo during these times, Lindo cunningly devises a way to capitalize on her in-laws' superstitious beliefs and fears of social taboo. She fabricates a vision using information that she has astutely observed to predict that her marriage is doomed unless it is immediately dissolved. Her in-laws believe her vision; they are all too willing to help her leave the household to avoid the bad omen and fate predicted by her vision to befall her husband. Thus, she is freed from her marriage without shame or ostracism; her in-laws gratefully send her away to Beijing if she promises not to tell her story, an unusual accomplishment during those times in China. It is her cleverness, resoluteness, and being true to herself that carry her through.

Lindo's daughter, Waverly, is considered crafty and snobbish like her mother. She is taught the "art of invisible strength" by her mother; that is, that the inner will is a dominant force. The mother-daughter relationship is a battle of the wills. As Lindo says, the strongest wind cannot be seen (referring to the winds in mahjong and martial arts). Waverly continues a silent battle with her mother over independence. Waverly develops her skills as a champion chess player in which she learns secret strategies from a neighbor. As she competes in tournaments and becomes the neighborhood heroine, she believes she is special (which is in contrast to the emphasis on modesty in Chinese culture). However, she is resentful of her mother's pride as an attempt to take credit for her accomplishments. When her mother modestly describes her winning as "luck," she views this as criticism.

She rebels after a confrontation, only to lose her mother's silent support. Without her mother's support, she gives up the chess game and loses interest in winning. She finally comes to terms with her battle for independence from her mother, realizing it has been a battle fought within herself. What she saw "as a formidable foe in her mother, was now simply an old woman waiting for her daughter to come home" (Tan, 1989).

Lindo and her daughter Waverly are born with the elements of wind—symbolizing strategy and invisible strength; their relationship emphasizes power and competition. Lindo's developmental transformation is her ability to give up the fight with her mother.

This contemporary novel of women in Chinese immigrant families differs from their depiction in classical Chinese stories in that it portrays mothers as human beings with faults. Its portrayal of mother–daughter bonds also differs from the tendency to portray cross-gender parent–child relationships (father–daughter, mother–son, and husband–wife) in classical Chinese stories.

In *The Joy Luck Club,* Chinese culture continues to pervade the characters' lives while creating conflict with the influence of American culture in their lives. The Chinese American mothers continue to use Confucian moral principles and threats in their childrearing techniques. Lindo uses open criticism of Waverly's accomplishment—a common demonstration of Chinese modesty—to elicit compliments; Waverly misunderstands her mother's maternal pride and modesty as simple criticism, illustrating a common intergenerational misunderstanding in immigrant families.

Unlike the *Twenty-Four Stories,* the emphasis on maternal guidance is cause for tension between mothers and daughters in *The Joy Luck Club.* As the daughters in this novel struggle for autonomy and identity, they rebel against maternal guidance and control. The mothers cannot understand the daughters' failure to abide by the mandate to be the obedient daughter.[3]

Each generation grapples with the same dynamic issues faced by their mothers before—symbolized by the elements with which they were born and that determine their fate. Despite their initial disdain and rebelliousness against maternal expectations, the daughters come to realize how perceptive their mothers are and come to value what they have gained. The process is transforming in establishing their bicultural identity and mother–daughter bonds.

The themes of loss and abandonment in An-Mei's story and the warrior images in Lindo's story are powerful cultural symbols and developmental themes as each negotiates the task of maturation.

WESTERN MYTHS OF ASIAN WOMEN

The contemporary portrayals of Chinese American women in *The Joy Luck Club* and *The Woman Warrior* are more popular among Chinese Americans because they emphasize women's strengths and end with admiration and pride, unlike many portrayals popular among Westerners about Asian women, including *Madame Butterfly, Sayonara,* and *Miss Saigon,* which portray Asian women as meek, subservient, and victimized. The latter stories end with pity for the heroine; they are tragedies whereby the Asian woman typically commits suicide following her unfulfilled union with the white male—that is, Asian women are abandoned and shamed. These stories mimic Asian values and are written from Western perspectives. Westerners often fail to understand that the latter portrayals victimize Asian women and deifies white men.

Other 20th-century stories about Asian women featured them as prostitutes and losers. These were initially popular among Asian audiences because so few movies featured Asian women as stars; they were later seen as offensive because they reinforced stereotypic myths and images about Asian women as subservient, exotic, and self-effacing while remaining immensely popular among Western audiences.

Madame Butterfly and Suzie Wong

Madame Butterfly (Puccini, 1904), *The World of Suzie Wong* (Quine, 1960), *Sayonara* (Logan, 1957), and *Miss Saigon* (Schönberg, Maltby, & Boublil, 1990) are examples of contemporary movies and plays about Asian women in the periods following World War II and the Vietnam War. While Western audiences extol the exotic beauty and innocence of the Asian woman, and forgive her for selling her body, they nonetheless pity her. She is pathetic because the white world is not hers to share; she is innocent and foolishly committed to the white male soldier. She is ultimately the transient toy and sexual object for the American soldier before he returns to the *real* woman who is the object of his affection; in other words, she is abandoned for the white woman back home. After the war, the white male moves on while the Asian female mourns his loss; in her anguish or shame over losing the white man's love, she commits suicide. This is the myth about Asian women that Western filmmakers love to portray; it is the image that Western audiences retain.

The characters of Butterfly and her Captain Pinkerton illustrate this myth in the opera of *Madame Butterfly* by Puccini (1904). Pinkerton, a dashing officer in the United States Navy, is also a philandering heel; he is infatuated with the 15-year-old Butterfly, cognizant of her fragility, but is not "content with life unless he makes his treasure the flowers on every shore." He says as he compares her to a butterfly, "I must pursue her even though I damage her wings." The stage for the tragedy is set. The beautiful Cio-Cio San has been a geisha, but is nonetheless fragile, unworldly, and in love with the handsome sailor. She deceives herself, despite abundant warnings, as to Pinkerton's motives.

This theme and myth about Asian women is repeated half a century later in the play *Miss Saigon* (Schönberg et al., 1990), which revolves around Kim, a young Vietnamese woman who is forced to work in a sex shop in Saigon. She quickly falls in love with Chris, a marine guard at the U.S. embassy. When Saigon falls to the Viet Cong, Chris—not realizing that Kim is pregnant—is forced to retreat and abandon her. He returns home and eventually marries a white woman. A few years later, he and his wife return to find Kim, who is now determined to make Chris take their son back to the United States. Realizing her shame, she commits suicide to die with honor.

Suzie Wong—the very name offends a generation of Asian Americans who grew up in its shadow. While many today have not actually seen *The World of Suzie Wong,* the 1960 movie directed by Richard Quine, what matters is that after the film's release the most superficial (and offensive) aspects of the Suzie Wong character singlehandedly usurped the image of Asian womanhood in the Western imagination. Robert Lomax is a struggling American artist who has moved to Hong Kong to learn whether he can really paint. He meets Mee Ling, a tycoon's beautiful daughter, onboard Hong Kong's Star Ferry. After checking into a local Wan Chai hotel, he learns that the hotel is actually a brothel, and that Mee Ling is actually Suzie Wong, the most popular prostitute in the place. Refusing to accept Suzie because of her way of life, Robert's relationship with Suzie begins as a purely artistic one, then becomes platonic friendship, then anger tinged with hidden jealousy and internal conflict, then passionate love, and finally an acceptance of her as a complete person, but not without tragic consequences. In the Asian American consciousness, the two most offensive images are Suzie Wong and Madame Butterfly because they degrade Asian women as prostitutes and insult Asian men by implying that only Caucasian men are worthy objects of love (Nahm, 2003). They marginalized and placed into bondage the women they defined; Chinese American women were called "Suzie" for years after the movie's release.

BICULTURAL IDENTITY:
BE CHINESE! YOU ARE AN AMERICAN!

The Chinese emphasize the importance of being Chinese in their childrearing, while our American culture emphasizes the importance of being American—this is the contradiction.

The Flower Drum Song

The Flower Drum Song was one of the first contemporary movies to portray Asian women and men in positive roles and positions of strength in a musical romantic comedy. Mei Li, a sweet, modest Hong Kong picture bride arrives to marry Sammy Fong, a nightclub owner who is in love with Nancy Low, a sultry, brassy showgirl. The contrasts between the women as "traditional" versus "modern" capture the dichotomous images of Chinese American women and the essence of achieving a cultural identity. Mei Li falls in love with Ta, who is more interested in Nancy Low, much to his father's disapproval of her "less traditional" image. As the couples struggle with their choice of a mate in marriage, the challenges of biculturalism are played out.

As Ta's father insists, the mandate to be Chinese and to pick the perfect Chinese wife is strong—embodied in Mei Li. Yet as Sammy Fong and Nancy Low realize, they are who they are, influenced by Western ways. Unfortunately, the story reinforces the notion that there is a forced choice to be either Chinese or to be American, instead of showing the ability to evolve a strong bicultural identity.

CREATING IMMIGRATION LEGENDS

The Joy Luck Club, The Woman Warrior, and *The Flower Drum Song* offer more favorable images of Chinese women as they illustrate the challenges faced by Chinese American immigrant families as they assimilate into Western society. *Crouching Tiger, Hidden Dragon* draws on Chinese legend and symbols to provide meaning for life's journey in today's terms. These contrast with stories that perpetuate a myth that the Chinese would never be allowed to rise in a white man's world. This was illustrated in the stories of *Madame Butterfly* and *The World of Suzie Wong,* which created the Western myths and degrading images about Asian women while celebrating their beauty, innocence, and modesty.

The difference between the stories written from Asian perspectives and by Asian writers (i.e., *Crouching Tiger, Hidden Dragon* and *The Joy Luck Club*) was in their ability to capture the complexity of Chinese values and beliefs, and to celebrate the strengths of Chinese culture and Chinese immigrant families. These become the immigration legends that sustain immigrant families as they journey forward, bond together, and develop a bicultural identity.

Having Face: Teaching Family Loyalty and Obligation

To look at creating legend, we should look at what Chinese immigrant families teach. A core principle is that one must *yu meen* ("have face"). Chinese immigrant families frequently reinforce this principle in their accusations and criticism that someone *hmn pa chew* ("is not afraid of shame") when someone brags or is too bold. This emphasis on shame is pervasive as a means for social control of behavior. It is shared in that an individual's shame or pride is not only felt; it is shared by the family (e.g., the family shame because the mother of An-Mei in *The Joy Luck Club* was raped).

A second core principle is that of family loyalty and maintaining a Chinese identity. Growing up Chinese American, children are taught to be proud of the 5,000 years of Chinese culture and achievements in comparison to the paltry 300 years of American culture. This emphasis was, in part, reactive to the emphasis on American patriotism and white middle-class norms in schools and society to the exclusion of the contributions of other cultures. (For example, Americans often teach American history as starting with the arrival of the Pilgrims on Plymouth Rock.)

Yet Chinese Americans growing up are always compared against white middle-class norms and questioned about how American they are; differences are viewed as deviant, exotic, or un-American. There is often an inherent assumption and expectation that immigrants moved along a continuum of acculturation to Westernization. There have been periods of explicit racist attitudes and policies that fueled the mistrust of early Chinese immigrants.

In drawing on mythology and stories of strength, we can create new legends among immigrant families that empower and heal. The abandonment and losses, the experience of racism, the conflicts of identity must all be captured in a family's legend as they make their journey to enlightenment.

GOLDEN MOUNTAIN MYTH: THE SEARCH

America the beautiful, the land of opportunity! These were the words heard by Toisanese Chinese immigrants. *Fah Kay* (Flowered Flag) or *Mei Kuo* (Beautiful Country) were the names that the Toisanese Chinese immigrants gave to the United States. The image of the U.S. was *Gum San,* or Golden Mountain. Chinese immigrants heard of the Golden Mountains in the hills of San Francisco during the California gold rush where, according to immigration myth, it was said that men could pick gold off the streets. The myth grew as the Chinese dreamed of immigrating to the Golden Mountain and returning to China as rich men. As the early Chinese sojourners toiled to build the railroads and mined the gold dust left behind by the white gold miners, they perpetuated the myth to their families back home. Their search for a fortune left them poor with few opportunities to return to China, much less as rich men. They embellished their stories of riches to themselves and to their wives, in order to ease the pain of poverty and racism faced here in America.

Melting Pot Myth: The American Dream

This vision of America in turn perpetuated the melting pot myth, the belief that we are one people, that we are an immigrant nation, and that this is a land of equal opportunity where all men are created equal, and you can become an American. It was a myth because in a race-conscious society, you need to be white and "look American" to enjoy the fruits of opportunity. Yet the melting pot myth was taught in schools and pounded into speeches. This denial that race doesn't matter created generations of Americans who doubted their identities and selves. It created the mistaken belief that if you did not get something, it was because you did not work hard enough. We came to realize that the "American dream" is limited to those who are white and that this needed to be rectified. The words of Martin Luther King, in his famous 1963 speech on the steps on the Lincoln Memorial, is the legend yet to be realized: "I have a dream deeply rooted in the American dream. I have a dream that this nation will rise up one day, and live out the true meaning of its creed. We hold these truths to be self-evident, that all men are created equal."

The New Colossus: Statue of Liberty

Not like the brazen giant of Greek fame,
With conquering limbs astride from land to land,

Here at our sea-washed, sunset-gates shall stand
A mighty woman with a torch, whose flame
Is the imprisoned lightning, and her name
Mother of Exiles. From her beacon-hand
Glows world-wide welcome, her mild eyes command
The air-bridged harbor that twin-cities frame.

"Keep, ancient lands, your storied pomp!" cries she,
With silent lips. "Give me your tired, your poor,
Your huddled masses yearning to breathe free,
The wretched refuse of your teeming shore;
Send these, the homeless, tempest-tost to me,
I lift my lamp beside the golden door!"

Emma Lazarus, November, 2, 1883

The "New Colossus," the famous sonnet written by Emma Lazarus in 1883, has been affixed to the inner walls on the pedestal of the Statue of Liberty since the early 1900s. It has come to symbolize the statue's universal message of hope and freedom for immigrants coming to America and people seeking freedom around the world. The Statue of Liberty is more than a monument; it is a legend. Called the "Copper Lady" by Chinese immigrants, it is one of the most universal symbols of political freedom and democracy. It is the gateway to New York City where many Chinese immigrants landed; it is the place where all the tourists go; it is the place from which the immigration legend begins. Yet the policies and practices of racial exclusion and anti-Asian legislation stands testimony to its contradiction.

CHAPTER 3

Cultural Symbols: Universal Bonds

Day by Day

The days of our lives fly by so freely,
Like the fresh morning air that feels like a sea breeze.
The moments that pass, feel the ecstasy that persists,
Wishing time would tell and always exist.

Growing an appreciation for quality time makes us aware. . .
Of how precious life's opportunities are to give and share.

Living, loving, sharing and giving make up
What the world should be all about.
Following the golden path of life's pleasures
Should lead us down that route.

We learn from our mistakes that may occur day by day,
And gain the knowledge that will never go astray.

Tracey Lynette Ong

FOOD SYMBOLS: BONDS BETWEEN PEOPLE

As a culture that stresses the use of metaphors and symbolism, food and
words become highly symbolic in capturing the essence of Chinese cul-

ture and its values. The contrasts between Chinese and American cultural symbols also illustrate the challenges that Chinese Americans face in creating a new bicultural identity as they grapple with issues of assimilation, self-esteem, and belongingness.

The Immortal Peach Versus the Forbidden Apple

In the Bible, it is Eve who tempts Adam to eat the forbidden fruit— the apple in the Garden of Eden in the East. In Taoism and Buddhism, it is Monkey who steals the peach of immortality and is banished from heaven (Jade Mountain of the West). The apple in the Garden of Eden is a symbol of earthly desires and temptation; it is a fruit from the tree of knowledge, and also represented Christ and the divine wisdom. The peach from the Jade Mountain of the West is a symbol of great importance in China; it symbolizes longevity and immortality. *T'ao*, the Chinese word for "peach," is a homonym for marriage; consequently, the peach is considered propitious for marriage. Because it blooms early, it also symbolizes fertility (Gibson, 1996).

From the time of creation, food has come to symbolize the bonds among people more than the sustenance needed to keep us alive and healthy. In the West, the emphasis is on earthly temptation and the relationship between man and woman. In the East, the emphasis is on immortality and the mother–son relationship.

Nurturing Our Bodies and Soul: A Journey

While food is often considered the universal bond, food rituals vary widely across cultures and have great significance in reflecting a culture's values and beliefs. Tea, for example, is common in the rituals of several cultures. The tea ceremony in Japanese culture is a sacred ceremony conducted in silence to honor an esteemed guest. *Dim sum* (little pleasures) or *yum cha* (tea-drinking time) in Chinese culture is ritualized as a Sunday brunch and time to make connections with family, friends, and relatives at the teahouses. High tea, taken during the afternoon in British culture, is typically accompanied by serving simple cookies or cake with a few friends.

Sharing a meal is a common bonding experience for people in most cultures. While Westerners "break bread together," Chinese will "eat rice together"; thus, "Have you eaten rice yet?" in Chinese is comparable to the American "Hello." Food is at the heart of our cultural rituals to celebrate our children, our ancestors, and our selves—through banquets in the Chinese culture. Birthday banquets generally have a dish of long noodles or *cherng mein*, meaning "long life," to promote longevity. The names of dishes or their ingredients are often homonyms for propitious characteristics; for example, we have dishes named *tze gee tau* or lion's head (i.e., pork balls); *chern ga fook* or entire family prosperity,; *bat bow fan* or eight precious treasures rice; yin yang rice; dragon and phoenix platter; and *fot gow* or prosperity cake. Good fortune befalls those who partake—to become healthy, wealthy, or wise. or it is offered Reverence is bestowed to those to whom it is offered, that is, our ancestors. And so it was in our family.

ANIMAL SYMBOLS: CHARACTER TRAITS

Animals are frequently used in Chinese culture to embody the traits they symbolize and to imbue the recipients with these traits. This is especially true in the martial arts where movements are named after animals as metaphors for the power they produce. People are believed to acquire the traits of the Chinese zodiac animal for the year in which they are born. Finally, the Chinese will eat an animal or its representation in order to acquire the traits associated with that animal.

Animal parts are also used for their healing properties in Chinese medicine and herbal tonics to restore health or to balance yin-yang qualities. Their value is enhanced depending on the specific conditions under which they are caught. For example, the value of deer antlers, used for herbal tonics, is increased if the deer is shot while running downhill, according to my mother. It is believed that all the blood and nutrients rush to its head and antlers when the deer runs downhill. We always asked my mother how the seller could prove this; she would tell us only that we needed to trust and believe.

Mythical Animals: Dragons, Phoenix, Tigers

The Chinese dragon is often seen as the symbol of divine protection and vigilance. It is regarded as the supreme being amongst all creatures. It has the ability to live in the seas, fly up to the heavens, and coil up in the land in the form of mountains. Being a divine mythical animal, the dragon can ward off wandering evil spirits, protect the innocent, and bestow safety to all that hold his emblem. The dragon is said to have nine resemblances; there are five types of dragons with the celestial dragon representing joy, health, and fertility. It is protective, in contrast to the Western image of the dragon as negative and satanic and representative of destructive power and a defiler of innocence.

The phoenix is considered to be the emperor of birds and one of the four sacred creatures whose presence appears in times of peace and prosperity; it remains hidden at other times, deriving its divine origin from the sun or fire connecting it with the south. The dragon and phoenix are frequently depicted together, personifying the unity of yin and yang, or male and female. The dragon is a male solar symbol representing happiness, while the phoenix is a female lunar symbol of the Chinese empress. Commonly used as a theme in wedding celebrations, the dragon and phoenix (served as lobster and chicken dishes) are linked as animals that bring happiness, health, and fertility.

Tigers are not native to China and so were treated as mythical beasts. The tiger is regarded to be the fiercest of beasts, and is also considered the king of all wild beasts—contrary to the West, where the lion is considered king of beasts. The stripes on its head are imagined to form the Chinese character *wang*, meaning king (Scott, 1980). Courageous, aggressive, and adventurous to extremes, the tiger is considered sensitive and generous to loved ones. Admired for its playful personality, it is compatible with dragons, horses, and dogs. In Chinese culture, the tiger represents vital animal energy, power, ferocity, royalty, and thus protection. The tiger protects graves and is a Chinese guardian of hunting. The white tiger has *yin* (female) attributes and opposes the dragon. Because it can see in the dark, it symbolizes illumination and the new moon. Tigers also have *yang* (male) attributes and signify the way and valor.

Thus, the tiger and dragon are symbols of opposing but complementary strength and power, as demonstrated in the movie, *Crouching Tiger, Hidden Dragon*, and of the hidden power and strength of Lindo Jong in *The Joy Luck Club*.

Earthly Animals: Turtle and Monkey

The turtle (or tortoise) in Chinese culture is believed to carry the world or to represent the cosmos; its upper shell represents the heavens, its body the earth, and the underside of its shell the water or underworld. It is a symbol of longevity, indestructibility, and immortality (Gibson, 1996). The monkey represents fantasy, intelligence, and cunning; he is a trickster figure embodying base human nature.

The Lion Dance: Dance for Good Fortune

The Chinese use the lion dance as a vehicle for dispensing the good blessings of heaven to the community and for guarding against misfortune. The dance is performed not only during the Lunar New Year celebration, but also on auspicious occasions (e.g., weddings) and represents the hopes and aspirations for all the good things that life holds. The lion dance (see http://a2amas.com/liondance/) begins in a cave, behind a closed portal, with a sleeping lion. An overweight Buddhist monk enters, looks around, and prepares the shrine. He lights a lantern, opens the portal's double doors, sweeps away the dust and leaves, and lights candles and incense burners. He wakens the lion with a drum and gong and they play.

Eventually the monk tries to entice the lion to pray before the altar, but the lion has other plans. When the lion gets bored, the monk teases him with some greens, which makes the lion angry, so he subsequently bites the monk. The lion then takes the greens from the monk and eats them. Sometimes additional greens are hung out of the lion's reach. The lion disperses the greens onto the audience three times, giving them the blessings of health, wealth, and good fortune. After a nap, the lion is ready to play again, but the monk has left, leaving the lion to dance by himself before backing into the cave.

In Chinese culture the lion is said to possess mystical properties. When paired with the five colors (yellow, black, green, red, and white) of his costume, the lion is said to have control over the five cardinal directions. The costume is composed of many symbolic shapes. The bird-shaped horn represents the phoenix. The ears and tail are of the unicorn. The protruding forehead, adorned with a mirror that deflects evil forces, and the long beard, are characteristic of Asian dragons. The lion walks back and forth, in a zigzag path, in order to confuse evil spirits, which the Chinese believe move in straight lines. Finally, the lion's act of eating and dispersing of the greens symbolizes the dispersing of wealth and good fortune to all who are present.

Chicken and Fish: Harmony and Completeness

As a child, I was sent to buy a fish once. The "fishman," as my mother would call him, removed the head while cleaning it. My mother was so upset that she sent me to return the fish; she considered it incomplete since it was not whole. I remember feeling mortified because I thought the fishman would laugh at me. To my great relief, the fishman understood and gave me another fish. My mother would always admonish us to finish our rice, especially during the Lunar New Year, since it would be a bad omen for the coming year if we didn't. Somehow it meant that something bad would happen to us. We never really knew what that would be, but we always complied. Then she would say that we would end up marrying a pock-faced husband if we didn't finish our rice.

This emphasis on wholeness and completeness symbolizes the importance of harmony in Chinese culture and the sense of imbalance and impending doom when it is not there. Only as an adult could I begin to appreciate how these rituals and practices helped to provide the feelings of security, integrity, and plenty in one's life. The ambivalent feelings we experienced as children were part of the bicultural struggle. It combined the sense of uniqueness and connection amidst the struggle of being viewed as different, exotic, or alien.

The harmony and balance necessary in life according to Chinese culture is often represented by the wholeness of the chicken we serve. It was always important in our family and other Chinese families to have a whole chicken at all celebrations and rituals. The bland and simple white chicken served during funeral dinners represents mourning, while the decorated or roasted chicken served during birthdays and weddings represents happiness and celebration. Although it was not customary or necessary for my parents to buy birthday presents for us as children, they were sure to serve a chicken to celebrate our birthdays. Unfortunately, we often preferred the present.

Fish is important in Chinese culture not only because it can be served whole, but also because the Chinese word for fish—*yau yee*—is a homonym for abundance. In eating fish, we would have abundance. Later on we discovered that fried squid or *chow yau yee,* pronounced in a slightly higher tone, might be used as a code to announce to the eater that he or she was going to be fired from his or her job. This play on words is common to Chinese eating habits and in the naming of food dishes.

RITUALS: PROMOTING HARMONY AND GOOD FORTUNE

Specific foods and dishes are often prepared symbolically to celebrate different Chinese festivals and to promote the qualities of harmony, balance, or prosperity. The eating of special foods is also cause for celebration to acquire the traits of various animals. I remember a special occasion when my parents and their friends had captured or bought a mountain lion. This animal was to be cooked for dinner. Because the Chinese always want their food to be at its freshest, the mountain lion was caged, waiting to be slaughtered as we cautiously approached to see it. As children, I remember our awe and limited understanding of the big fuss over this poor animal. We did not realize how rare the mountain lion was as a food item; nor did we appreciate the power of its traits of power, energy, and courage that would be acquired. The following excerpt captures the experience.

Drinking Tiger Soup

When I was six or seven, my mother's aunt gave me a broth made of tiger bone. She promised it would cure my asthma and turn me into a robust child. My mother, a great believer in ancient remedies, readily consented.

"You are lucky," Great Aunt told me, as she poured the steaming black broth into a bowl. "With all the bombings, there aren't that many tigers left in our country. You, boy, might be drinking the bones of the last one." Our country was Vietnam.

I watched the soup billowing smoke in front of me, and felt as if I was about to swallow poison. To make things worse, the tiger was my favorite animal and I was certain I was wholly unworthy to receive such a sacrifice. But a Vietnamese child is obedient; I wept, but I drank. (Lam, 1996)

Red Eggs Celebration: Creation

Upon the birth of a child, Chinese parents will often celebrate the 1-month birthday of the child, especially if it is a boy. Given the high rate of infant mortality in China, newborns and postnatal Chinese mothers stay at home for the entire month. Special tonics are prepared, including a special chicken soup spiced with gin and ginger, and pig trotters vinaigrette with eggs and peanuts to help the postpartum mother restore her strength. A 1-month birthday banquet may include the dish of red-colored eggs to symbolize the celebration of creation. The newborn receives monetary gifts in red envelopes, or 24-carat-gold jewelry from the relatives as wishes of happiness and prosperity.

The Chinese Wedding

The Chinese wedding is celebrated with the color red and many symbols of fertility, longevity, and harmony—to bear children, live a long life, and promote harmony between husband and wife. Growing up Chinese American, our means were modest and we struggled to make ends meet. Yet true to Chinese tradition, my mother was intent on buying jewelry for our dowry to make sure we would "have face" when we married. She emphasized fairness in always buying the same for my sister and me, always cautioning us never to fight among ourselves over material things. Two of her most treasured and classic pieces of jewelry were the 24-carat gold *lung fung* (dragon-phoenix) bangle bracelets and the jade heart. Almost every Chinese American bride gets one, and we were to be no different.

A camphor-type hope chest is also commonly part of the dowry among Chinese Americans. Since Chinese goods were less common in the United States and hard to find without paying a lot, it was common practice for immigrants arriving from China to make purchases for those who were already here. Consequently, my mother went through pains to ask relatives and friends arriving from China to purchase these items so that we would have a proper dowry. When my hope chest arrived, it turned out to be mahogany with mother of pearl inlaid depicting a dragon and phoenix. If I had to have a hope chest, I wanted a carved wood chest with a simple design. I initially hated its gaudiness, and at the time preferred the simplicity of Scandinavian design. I hated this chest so much that I covered it up, believing my mother just did not understand or have proper taste. Twenty years later, I found this chest to be quite beautiful, as it provides contrast and aesthetic interest against the plainness of my Scandinavian furniture.

These rituals, symbols, and our struggles are characteristically Chinese American. The celebration of Chinese weddings, in particular, illustrates the stark contrast and contradiction between Western and Chinese cultures. The white wedding gown, a symbol of purity and virginity in Western culture, stands in antithesis to the red satin embroidered wedding gown, a symbol of celebration and fertility in Chinese culture. In the West, red is flamboyant while in the East, white is for mourning.

There were several defining moments when we first began to celebrate weddings within the family. My sister, Fay Hah,[1] was the first to marry. We stood in awe when her future in-laws sent over a whole succulent roast pig, complete with the apple in the mouth, after the engagement as a symbol of their acceptance and pleasure with the future daughter-in-law. As a symbol of the prosperity and generosity of the groom's family, this was accepted with great pleasure by my parents. Another roast pig and a monetary dowry followed 3 days after the wedding to mark the first time the bride is traditionally allowed to return home to visit her parents.

At my brother Sel Teng's wedding, coconut heads were delivered to our family by the bride's family, along with other gifts as a way to honor my father as the new father-in-law and head of the family; coconut or *year how* in Chinese is a homonym for "father-in-law's head." We chuckled at the *double entendre* of these symbols. My future mother in-law was living in Hong Kong at the time of my wedding and could not be present at the ceremony; my husband and I were represented at the wedding banquet she held in Hong Kong by two chickens.

Other wedding customs include the presentation of a wild goose as the symbol of marital harmony and fidelity; these birds mate for life and migrate together. Because wild geese are difficult to obtain, chickens have been used as an alternative. Fruits and nuts are frequently offered as gifts to symbolize fertility and wishes for the couple to bear many children. Peanuts (*sheng*), a homonym for birth, and dates (*zaozi*), a homonym for "early arrival of a male son" are often placed inside the new quilt on the marital bed.

Lunar New Year: Family Bonds

The Lunar New Year Festival is a time of great celebration in Chinese culture, more important than Christmas or Thanksgiving in American culture. Celebrations will continue for several weeks with visits to friends and relatives bearing pastries and sweets made especially for Lunar New Year. If symbolism is important in the eating customs among Chinese, it is even more the case during the Lunar New Year. Great preparation is needed to bring in the New Year. One must have a clean house and clean body; one must resolve all debts; one cannot do chores on New Year's Day.

My mother would spend weeks preparing the pastries, as would all the other Chinese American mothers and grandmothers. We would spend hours together kneading the dough and forming the wrappers to be filled with sugar and peanuts (*fah sheng*), symbolizing sweet "life." A popular New Year dessert is *nien gao*, a sweet steamed glutinous rice pudding, a homonym for the "year will soar high." My mother often made extra pastries, especially for the men whose wives were not in the United States to make it for them. I have memories of how she would beam with pride when she was complimented about how good they tasted; yet she would modestly claim that they were only so-so.

Lunar New Year is a time of constant feasting with dishes symbolizing longevity, prosperity, and happiness. New Year's Eve is a night of feasting, while New Year's Day is a day of fasting, that is, eating *lo horn ji*, a vegetarian dish made out of respect for all living animals. It is expected that one must have only good thoughts, have no arguments, finish all of one's rice, and be especially careful not to break anything in order to usher in the New Year. We would comply to ensure that the year would be propitious and that no harm would befall us. My parents, as did all of our relatives, always gave us *hung bao* (red envelopes) filled with money on New Year's Day to wish us prosperity and good fortune.

Following New Year's Day, all families must officially *hoy neen,* or open the year by having a dinner banquet for family and friends. On this occasion, my father always emphasized how we only used *jing sick toy lieu* (the most genuine of ingredients) in creating the dishes. He would proudly claim how we did not scrimp on ingredients in our home cooking the way they did in restaurants; we used only the best ingredients. Rituals were followed in preparing this ten-course banquet. Special dishes were served, each one a homonym for some auspicious wish for prosperity, happiness, or longevity; and each one symbolizing some desirable trait. Before sitting down to dinner, the food is presented as a sacrifice before the picture of our ancestors. There was the dish with black fungus or *fot toy* symbolizing prosperity; the bean curd dish or *foo juk* to take away the bitterness; the *see yoo* or radish dish to make our events turn out well; the vermicelli or *fun see* dish so that we might all find our fortune; and jujubes or *hung do* dish to celebrate the happiness. Of course, we could not do without the whole chicken and fish to symbolize unity and wholeness, or a "favorable start and finish."

As children, we loved and looked forward to Lunar New Year. Every year, my mother would explain once again the meaning of each of the different foods used to prepare the Chinese New Year dinner. Each year, we would listen as if it were the first time. There were to be no unpleasant words or thoughts. If any of us said something inauspicious by accident, she would say, *"Chick gaw lai see,"* a Chinese version of *gezunheit* to neutralize the bad thought. All of this meant so much to my mother, and ultimately to all of us, as she emphasized the completeness and circularity of life. She frequently reminded us of how every person comes full circle, and follows in the footsteps of one another.

My mother never fully knew the customs in detail, not having had her own mother for much of her childhood; however, she kind of made them up along the way. When we would question a practice or symbol in too much detail, she would resort to saying, "Let's just say it is good." She would often explain that it was to have *yuan,* a word for "roundness" suggesting the attainment of what are commonly known as the five happinesses: long life, wealth, peace, virtue, and honor. It also suggests family unity and harmony, and the unity of society; this was her goal.

Christmas and Thanksgiving, on the other hand, were just ordinary days since these holidays bore little significance in the Chinese culture. As we got older, we insisted on celebrating it "just like everybody else." Then my mother decided we would celebrate by serving a fresh-killed whole chicken. As we got older, my sister and I decided to celebrate Christmas ourselves, and began our own custom of exchanging presents. We decorated a small, artificial Christmas tree; we too made up our own rules. We always opened our presents soon after we got them instead of waiting for Christmas. Then we would carefully rewrap them and keep them under the tree until Christmas. My mother tolerated these Western holidays for our sake; at her suggestion, we began to keep the presents wrapped under the Christmas tree until February to celebrate Lunar New Year. We never thought this was odd; we were just being Chinese American.

Celebrating Our Ancestors: In the End

Food rituals continue until death—the end of the journey. In Chinese culture, there is often not a hard line drawn between the sacred and secular, or between our earthly world and that of the gods. (This was true in the adventures of Monkey King.) In honoring spirits, gods, and ancestors, the Chinese offer the same things that are useful in real life—food, entertainment, and money (Stepanchuck & Wong, 1991). Chinese American immigrants often altered these ceremonies to suit their new bicultural environment.

My mother was neither Buddhist nor Taoist; she supported the tenets of Christianity, since she saw them as being like Confucian moral teachings. After my father died, she created a shrine in his honor. She hung a large picture of my father over a table with Buddhist offerings, as is customary. She periodically began to *baishen,* or "worship the spirits," as a way to honor her ancestors Ah Gung, my grandfather; Dai Q, my maternal uncle; and my father after his death. Her practices were not "authentic" and were often modified for convenience; however, they gave her peace and fulfilled her sense of obligation and loyalty to the family and my father. It puzzled us at first. Later we realized it was the only way she knew to memorialize what she had. Not uncommon among Chinese American immigrants, she practiced these customs with more vigor and enthusiasm than even those in China.

In Chinese culture, a bland ten-course meal follows the end of the funeral for all mourners; the family will host this meal, asking all mourners to join in a meal of *white* rice (as mentioned previously, white is the color of mourning among the Chinese). Instead of the brightly colored dishes typical at banquets, a funeral meal will feature among its dishes a whole "white" chicken (i.e., poached chicken), "white" pastry, and the burning of incense in order to respect the deceased.

The Chinese honor their ancestors in an annual journey in April to the cemetery during the *Qing Ming* festival, which means "clear and bright as a day of remembrance." It corresponds with the onset of warmer weather, and the start of spring plowing. Families will tidy up the graves, remove weeds, and sweep away leaves. While Westerners bring flowers, the Chinese bring feasts to the ancestral graves as their offerings; they then have a picnic as part of this family outing.

THE CHINESE BANQUET:
BECOMING HEALTHY, WEALTHY, AND WISE

The Chinese banquet is traditional and full of ritual, intended to demonstrate abundance by the number and quality of dishes, generosity of its host, harmony and balance in the choice of dishes, and bonding in its execution and decorum.

The value placed on harmony and balance in Chinese culture is played out in the banquet—perfected to an art form. In a perfect Chinese banquet, all the dishes are in harmony with one another, balancing ingredients, tastes, and order of presentation. Ingredients in a dish are balanced in color, texture, shape, and flavor. There are nine or ten dishes symbolizing longevity or supreme; the lobster and chicken dishes are served in the middle (according to Cantonese cuisine), symbolizing the juxtaposition of the dragon and phoenix and the balance of yin-yang properties.

As children, we followed these customs and practices; we enjoyed the banquet food, but did not understand the full meaning of the various foods. As adults, we came to believe they would make us healthy, wealthy, and wise.

Yin and Yang: Health

In Chinese culture, the feminine principle of yin is described as a dark, moist, shadowy, and receptive power (i.e., the moon), that is creative, while the masculine principle of yang (i.e., the sun) is described as a bright, hot, powerful creative energy. Balance of these principles or energy is essential to life; it is the yin that brings all the yang stirrings into manifestation. Purging and fasting has been used to balance these energies within a person, and to drive out evil spirits or bad winds, which cause illness. Western cultures associate mother earth and heavenly father as feminine and masculine opposing principles. Healing in Asian cultures involves the restoration of bodily health, while healing in Western culture is the excision and suppression of disease. For Chinese, this means restoring the yin–yang balance through the use of herbal soups and tonics.

Prosperity and Fate (*Herng Fook*): Wealth

Owning land is a measure of prosperity in Chinese culture. My father bought a half-acre of land in Islip, New York, way out on Long Island. Since we rarely ventured outside New York City, this was "the country"; he was going to get us out of the ghetto. He was going to build a country home; this land was the promise of a dream that would remain unfulfilled. While he never built on this land, it symbolized his attainment of prosperity here in America.

Growing up, our living quarters were modest and small, as is the case for most Chinese immigrants. At family and social events, this meant that children were generally within earshot of the conversation of our elders. We were educated indirectly from listening to these conversations about *tiel meng*, or one's life and fate, and how some people were *ji-woon* (unlucky) while others were *herng-fook* (prosperous). Not much could be done about fate. The elders endlessly bemoaned their fate in America, struggling to make a living. Amidst this anguish were their dreams of returning to China in retirement to live in comfort and with respect in their home villages. This was the perpetual dream of my father as he and others hoped to make the hardship and struggle of working in a laundry more bearable. The elders would commiserate together, believing there was no escape from their fate of struggle and poverty, a kind of bondage. The dream of returning to an idyllic China with the most tasty and fresh fruit and the most beautiful flowers and scenery that far surpass any in America was the illusion of the peach orchard in the Jade Mountain of their minds.

It was the dream of my father and that of the Chinese elders not to toil so hard in laundries 12 hours a day 6 days a week, and to return to China in their retirement while they criticized the injustices of American society. As children, we would pooh-pooh my father, always challenging him, never believing him. Tired of hearing these empty dreams, we would tell him, "Why don't you go back; you'll hate it there," never realizing his bondage and his inability to escape his fate here in America. In 1972, at the age of 72, he made his trip back to China after almost

40 years; he found he no longer belonged. He returned with failing health, his dreams dashed, and died 2 years later.

In an immigrant community where most were poor, small differences were often important markers of social status. Many Toisanese immigrants had come with few of their possessions; most had little of value to bring. Jewelry was a means of demonstrating one's prosperity. As peasants born in poverty, 24-carat gold was valued not only for its monetary value, but also for its ability to be converted to cash. Unlike paper money, gold was not subject to depreciating value as a result of political and government turmoil. Twenty-four carat gold in the form of jewelry was a means of demonstrating one's prosperity as well as providing nuggets of security since it could be melted down in times of need.

The jade heart is often one of the first gifts of jewelry that Chinese immigrant mothers give to their daughters. In Chinese culture, jade is often worn as an amulet to protect one from harm and evil; it is believed to have protective powers. My mother always told the story of a woman who fell from a two-story window; the jade she was wearing broke but she was unharmed. My mother ensured that gold and jade would be part of our dowry, as did most Chinese immigrant mothers.

The power of these maternal gifts is immensely symbolic. When I was a young teen, a man exposed himself to me while I was traveling on a New York City subway. Frightened by the experience, my mother gave me a wad of black pepper wrapped in wax paper secured with a rubber band (this was before the days of pepper spray). I was told to throw this in someone's face if I was ever threatened again. For years, I walked around with this gift from my mother in my pocketbook with the illusion of feeling safe and protected. It was not until many years later that I wondered what I would have said if assaulted: "Wait, I have to get this pepper out of my bag so that I can mace you." By the time I opened my bag, found the pepper, removed the rubber band, and threw it in the person's face as I had been instructed to do, it would probably have been too late. But it was my mother's words and the symbol of her protection that made me feel safe.

Diligence (*Qin*) and Industry: Wisdom

Given the hardships of the laundry (and now the restaurants), Chinese parents placed their hopes and dreams on their children. While the opportunity for them to escape the laundry was viewed as futile, they placed their faith on a better future for their children.

And so we were told by my parents to study industriously, or *keen let duk shee,* so that we would not have to suffer working in a laundry. To be as wise as the scholars in China would bring respect and economic rewards. Books and the pursuit of academic achievement were valued. Because scholarly study was typically reserved for men, it was difficult for my parents to understand as I went on for my doctorate. My father expected me to go to work after I finished high school, and to contribute financially to the family until I married. This was their pension, since there was no social security in China.

At each step of my academic progress toward a higher degree, my parents expressed a mix of surprise, dismay, and pride. My father pondered the futility of an education for females if they were only to get married and have children; but then, this was America! At the same time, becoming a scholar was considered the height of achievement. But then, what was psychology anyway? When I first tried to explain to my mother in Chinese why my education was taking so many years, and what psychology was, she finally smiled. "Oh, you are going to be a brain surgeon," she said, since I had explained that psychology was going into the mind to examine and heal.

My parents' contradictory outlook and quandary reflected the challenges faced by Chinese immigrant families in a racist society. Many resorted to academic and scholarly pursuits, which fit with Confucian values, as a means of social and economic advancement. Our concise verbal styles, which were valued in Chinese culture, together with learning English as a second language channeled many toward the sciences and engineering.

WOMEN AS HEALERS

Chinese American immigrants continued the legacy of using food to celebrate and to cope with loss. Chinese immigrant women replicated the foods and food practices they had in China—in the herbal tonics for healing, pastries to celebrate Chinese New Year, and with the simple family meal. In feeding the family, they held the family together, advised their children, and promoted psychological, physical, and spiritual well-being.

Food as Health

Chinese soups, made from herbs and chicken, are considered tonics, which provide yin-yang properties and health benefits such as restoring balance to body fluids. So my mother created the soups to heal our bodies and nurture our souls through illness and suffering; she gave her gift of water to nurture and heal us, for us to fertilize and grow. Whenever we got cold sores or a cold, my mother would quickly boil some *lerng tong* (yin or cool tonic) for us to eliminate the *yeet hay* (hot air). If she thought us to be *yerk* (weak) or unhealthy, she might *oon* (long, slow braising) some ginseng, deer antlers, or other terrible-tasting tonic. If we had a fever, out came the *kam woo* tea to bring it down. She would apply a camphor salve and have us sweat it out; my mother, like most Chinese families, believed that the Western tradition of bringing a fever down with a tepid bath would kill us.

Health Tonics

Herbal soups (*yerk toy tong*) and tonics have played a distinct role in the healing practices within Chinese families. Basic essences of the body include *qi* (air), blood, and yin and yang qualities, which must be kept in balance in order to remain healthy. These are followed by the pathologic factors of wind, moisture, and toxins, which cause illness. Deficiencies of yin will give rise to symptoms of dryness (e.g., dry mouth and cough) and heat (e.g., fever and inflammation), while deficiencies of yang give rise to symptoms of poor vitality and strength (e.g., fatigue and impotence) and lack of adequate warmth (e.g., chills). Deficiencies are caused by the failure of one to regulate the other (yin-yang).

Herbal soups are routinely served as part of a family meal. The yin, associated with water and female qualities, are used to balance an overabundance of yang, associated with fire and male qualities. Thus, the essence of female was transmitted through these herbal soups, providing nurturance to strengthen and restore vitality and health. While herbalists, who are commonly men, are known for their significant role as healers in traditional and Chinese American communities, it has been the women or wives and mothers who regularly prepared these soups. Loo and Yu (1984), in a 1979 survey of health practices among Chinese Americans in San Francisco, found that this practice was highly prevalent; 95% of the respondents drank soups made with Chinese herbs; 23% drank them at least once a week, and 27% drank them at least once a month.

Since many Chinese immigrated from environments where infant mortality was high and starvation a reality, these tonics and soups provided their families with a means for dispelling evil spirits, toxins, and bad winds that cause ill health. Though we were skeptical as we drank the tonics and ate the food, we felt that much stronger as we incorporated the characteristics my mother imparted in wishing us health, wealth, and wisdom. Like the mooncakes we offered up to celebrate the August Moon Festival, we celebrate the moon as a reflection of female essence and symbolic of the great mother, who is also considered to be the great rain giver. Farmers and seafaring people, as the Toisanese were, believe the weather changes with each new moon, when the moon passes the full phase. Moon goddesses were regarded as guardians of the waters gushing forth out of the ground; they so aptly symbolize the invisible hidden power of "bringing forth from within," which is the peculiar characteristic of feminine creation (Harding, 1971).

WORDS AS SYMBOLS: A STUDY OF CONTRASTS

Words of a language often capture the essence of a culture and its values. Whether it is the names of dishes in a Chinese banquet or in a Chinese poem, the use of metaphor and symbolism in the Chinese language is high. There is an emphasis on brevity and the balance of words used to express scholarly thought and moral teaching.

Words: The Sayings of Confucius and Mencius

Though she was not a Chinese scholar, my mother repeated the sayings of Mencius and Confucius to me. Like most Chinese American children, I heard her warnings, her advice, her wisdom, and her moral teachings. Like the foods she prepared, her words symbolized the dreams to which so many Chinese Americans aspire and the longing for what they left behind. I heard her voice.

Confucius and Mencius were Chinese philosophers in the 5th and 4th centuries B.C.; both significantly influenced social and family relationships within Chinese culture. Confucius' sayings were both the object of awe and ridicule by Westerners. Picking up on the most superficial features of Confucianism, the Charlie Chan[2] version of Confucian wisdom stereotyped American images of this Chinese philosopher. Yet Confucian teachings were the basis for moral teachings in most Chinese American households.

Confucius' teachings were practical and ethical, rather than religious; they emphasized morality and proper social conduct based on the five virtues of kindness, uprightness, decorum, wisdom, and faithfulness, which constitute the whole of human duty, as described earlier in the *Twenty-Four Stories of Filial Piety*—one of his key concepts. Government and family relationships were paternalistic, with an emphasis on *li*, or ritual.

According to Confucius, there are five basic relationships in society that determines moral action and obligation: emperor–subject, father–son, husband–wife, elder brother–younger brother, elder friend–younger friend. All relationships are between a superior and inferior and demand obedience; a person needs to learn proper behavior for one's role. Through obedience, all upheld the proper distribution of power and authority (see http://beatl.barnard.columbia.edu/reacting/china/confucianism.html#philosophy).

Mencius (372–289 B.C.) argued that all men have a mind that cannot bear to see the suffering of others. As a disciple of Confucius, he added compassion to moral education. His teachings assert that feelings of commiseration, shame, modesty, and approval/disapproval are essential to human beings because of their compassion. Mencius asserted that these feelings are correlated with principles of behavior and social conduct: commiseration is the principle of benevolence; shame is the principle of righteousness; modesty is the principle of propriety; approval/disapproval is the principle of knowledge.

Style: Brevity Is the Soul of Wisdom

Spring couplets are verses used by the Chinese to bestow good fortune, longevity, or the birth of male offspring. Rules for composing a couplet are simple, but the art of composing these antithetical verses is a challenge. A couplet is made up of two lines of verse which are called the "head" and "tail," respectively, and should correspond with each other phonologically and syntactically word for word and phrase for phrase. For example,

> By virtue united, heaven is strong *(de he gan geng)*
> Through compassion shared, earth is yielding *(ci tong kun shun)*

The parallels between "virtue" and "compassion," "heaven" and "earth," "united" and "shared," and "strong" and "yielding" serve the same purpose, and may be opposite in meaning. The brevity and concentrated meaning of the couplet is uniquely Chinese. It leaves out more than it says; through the visual quality of characters, it reveals a hidden dimension, which readers have to puzzle out themselves (Stepanchuck & Wong, 1991).

This emphasis on brevity, metaphor, and balance is the hallmark of Chinese scholarship. As children, we were taught not to be too chatty, because virtuous women do not chat too much. We were cautioned to be quiet because "it did not look right," or that people would think "we had no shame." This contrasts with the Western standard in education, which expects us to raise our hands, speak up, and fight to be heard. We were taught that learning was a process of taking in information and listening; only fools did the opposite.

Scholarship in Western culture, by contrast, is often based on length and verbosity. While Westerners say, "A picture is worth a thousand words," the Chinese might say, "A word could say a thousand things." Consequently, a couplet of eight words in Chinese could say more than eight paragraphs in English.

The Power of Words: Chinese Names

What is in a name? We all have family names; for Westerners, it is a "last" name, while for Asians, it is placed first. Names have great symbolic significance in Chinese; they are chosen for their meaning to signify a character trait or a hope. Names typically have two radicals, with siblings sharing the same first radical to reflect their relationship; the second radical is distinctive, but may share a phrase across generations to reflect the ancestral bond.

Chinese have a tradition of giving names to mark important transition points in one's life. At times, it symbolizes an attempt to change our fate, to bring prosperity in times of adversity, or to bring hope where there is none. Names mark the essence of our identities; as Chinese Americans, we have our Chinese names and our American ones. As children, we always understood and felt the differences in the names we were called. We took on the different characteristics, behaviors, and values associated with our different names.

And so, my mother was called Tel as a child; she changed her name to May Yee after she had lost her mother under the former name. She used Jung Fung Gor, her paper name,[3] with Americans, while she was either Lee Tai (Mrs. Lee) or Lau Tai (Mrs. Lau) as my father's wife in Chinese; but she always identified herself as Wong May Yee (her maiden name), since this was who she was. She changed her American name to Fung Gor Jung Lee or Fung Gor Lee after my father died.

My father had even more names. Born as Ben On, he took on Yew Ock to mark his entry into adulthood. During his life, he kept both surnames of Lau and Lee out of respect and obligation to his birth and adopted families. His paper name was Kim Lau while he chose Louis

Tong as his first business name and Louis Kim when he ventured on to open a new laundry. He finally became Kim Lau Lee after he "confessed" following the Family Reunification Act of 1965; he kept this name until his death. If you add the different spellings to the Lau and Lee surnames because of different dialect pronunciations and changes made by immigration authorities upon entry to the United States, we can each claim several more names.

My parents gave us all nicknames, a typical Chinese custom to mark a particular character trait. Our tenants who were often late in paying their rent were called *heem do,* meaning "owe rent." My sister was called *gai na Ha,* meaning "Ha, the hen" for her spirited fights to protect her rights. Nicknames were not always complimentary as my father called me *pi gay por,* or "beggar woman," since I often did not fit standard size clothing because of my size.

What's in a name? It denotes our lineage; it marks our milestones; it denotes different parts of our identity. In Western culture, the emphasis on integration is paramount to our identity. In Chinese culture, there is not the need to bring it all together. After times of adversity, after major milestones, but most importantly because of the contrasting worldviews between Chinese and American culture, it is sometimes better to keep aspects of our identity apart. Instead of pathologizing this splitting, perhaps we can and do have multiple selves that can exist amidst multiple contexts, that is, in our Chinese American identities.

Part II

Biculturalism: Contrasts Between Cultures

As we examine Chinese mythology and contemporary storytelling, the themes in Chinese mythology mirror the life experiences of Chinese American immigrants, and are used to capture the immigrant experience. Life is a journey, and the immigrant experience highlights a journey with added challenges of uprooting and transplanting to a new and different culture. It is the thesis of this book that as immigrants make this journey and tell their stories, they create new legends about the cycle of life to sustain them and to nurture their children. These immigration legends become part of their group's identity. Each family creates its own immigration legend to preserve its history. This legend is communicated to future generations.

Part II of this book uses oral history to capture this story for a Chinese American family. This family saga describes an immigration journey and the influence of mythology and cultural symbols in its daily life. While this is a story of one family (see the table on page 64 for a list of names and honorific titles of the people involved in my family's story), other immigrant families might identify with the themes of abandonment and loss, trauma and survival, guilt and obligation, and journey and rebirth. In this immigration journey, the bonds we create and the bondage from which we cannot escape are the challenges and trials not unlike those made by the Monkey King in his journey to the west.

This use of oral history captures the subjective experience and the psychological dilemmas of the immigration experience. It shows defining moments—those transformative moments in our individual lives—that establish our cultural identities and self-identities. This section is told in my mother's voice to capture the effect of Chinese American immigrants living in a bicultural environment. Some of the stories in this oral history were retold many times by my parents during our childhood—their purpose in retelling being to teach, to heal, and to cope.

What happens when an Asian American daughter achieves middle-class educational and economic status, and in doing so, attains a social standing never dreamed of by her immigrant mother? How does an Asian American daughter establish a mother-daughter bond when she cannot fathom the trauma of separation, abandonment, and death experienced by her immigrant mother because of war, poverty, and immigration? How does an Asian American immigrant mother adapt to the world in which her daughter lives and advise her of that which she has not experienced? As Chinese American women face the challenges of stereotypic images of Asian women, of surviving amidst cultures of poverty and racism, of coping with contrasting expectations from Western and Chinese cultures, they are the women warriors of today. They must fight the battle to assert their place while being perceived as modest or exotic. They must fight the battle to enter an arena that may be closed. As mothers and daughters, they share an emotional bond that can transcend generational differences. Together, they can create the immigration legend that transforms the future.

While the differences between Western and Chinese cultures are significant, the plight of all Americans has been to make this journey and fight the battle, for there are few among us who can claim not to have descended from foreign shores, and struggled to be liberated on American soil.

Name	Honorific Title	Relationship to Author
Wong Shee Chew	*Ah Gung*	Maternal Grandfather
Kim Lau Lee	*Papa*	Father
Wong Tung Guey	*Dai Q*	Eldest Maternal Uncle
Wong Mei Yee		Mother's Maiden Name
Fung Gor Lee		Mother's Paper Name
	Ah Por	Maternal Grandmother
	Dai Kim	Maternal Aunt
Wong Chun Hoy	*Poy Q*	Maternal Uncle Poy
Wong Hing	*Hing Q*	Maternal Uncle Hing
	Cheung Por	Maternal Great Aunt
	Ah Nerng	Maternal Great Stepmother
Wong Gim Hing	*Ah Yee*	Maternal Aunt
Lee Kok Nong		Mother's first-born son
Lee Sel Ming	*Ming Gor*	Elder Brother
		Paper Maternal
Oliver Finds	*Kai Gung*	Grandfather
Willie Lau	*Ah Gor*	Elder Brother
Anna Ong	*Ah Jeer*	Elder Sister
Scott Chin		Son
Stephen Chin		Son
Wong Fei Gong		Maternal 1st cousin

CHAPTER 4

Of Survival and Striving: An Intergenerational Saga

My Special Mom

I admire the strength that possesses my mom
All the things she deals with and is still able to remain calm

The warmth and precious thoughts that we may feel,
Are comforting to the heart and are very real

Her words of wisdom that have advised me through and through,
Have given me a point of direction that I never knew.

No matter how I feel, she brings a smile to my lips,
With power that is unforgettable like a tidal wave that rips.

The link between us will always be together,
As mother and daughter, our love will be forever.

Tracey Lynette Ong

IN THE BEGINNING: THE FLOODS

According to the ancient Chinese myth of the great flood, the moon goddess sent her representative to earth, after the waters had subsided, to repopulate the world. The Chinese moon goddess, after the flood, gave birth to all living things. It is a renewed world and a new creation. Men, women, and all animals arise from the different parts of her person. Not only is she the life giver; she is also the destroyer. She creates all life on earth, and then comes the flood, which overwhelms it. And this flood is her doing, for she is the cause of rain and storm, of the tide and also of the flood. But she laments over their consequences, and does her best to save her children, who have all become "like the fishes of the sea" (Harding, 1971, p. 109).

And with the floods came the Toisanese Chinese immigrants to America. From tiny farming villages in the southern part of Canton Province in China came scores of peasants immigrating to the shores of the United States during the early 1900s. The floods of the Pearl River had devastated the land. Driven by the scourges of poverty, striving toward the fruits of prosperity, seeking to return as respected men to their families in China, they came in search of the golden mountain. The mountains of San Francisco gleamed with gold as they beckoned across oceans. Their shimmer behind the setting sun of the West embodied dreams from the East. They belied the darkness of the tunnels and railroads, of the sweat and toil that lay ahead.

With the Toisanese immigrants came their hopes for a life of splendor, reminiscent of emperors, a sure escape from the certainty of starvation. Alas, with them also came their differences of culture and language, of values and lifestyles, which thrust them into a world of indifference, a sea of racism that kept them oceans apart from their neighbors next door. They came, separated from their homeland, leaving behind loved ones. They lived alienated from the mainstream, yearning to return home to China; they survived in America.

AN INTERGENERATIONAL SAGA: IN MY MOTHER'S VOICE

Through the voice of my mother, we can hear anguish—the anguish of loss, abandonment, and guilt. Through her eyes, we can see the world in its vastness, separated by oceans and yet so small. Her life in America was confined to New York City's Chinatown of five long blocks along Mott Street with a one-mile radius. My mother was Toisanese, an immigrant. As she aged, her voice grew loud as she lost her hearing in one ear and was reduced to 10% hearing in the other. Her voice cried out on ears too hurried to hear stories frozen in time and place while the world moved on. Her Chinese words struggled to reach English ears, unable or sometimes too arrogant to give them their due. Her world was confined by the limitations of her hearing; we would bemoan the isolation she must have felt. How much the alienation of cultures between East and West, or the need to preserve what she left behind, left her content to close herself to the new worlds we now sought, we will never know. We do know how sometimes, her world, rich in imagination, drew upon the depth of her experience to make up for what she could not or chose not to hear. She was an active and energetic woman until her death.

When I left my mother's home to follow my professional and personal pursuits, I left New York City where I was born and moved to Boston, a distance of 250 miles. For years, at the end of each of our visits together, my mother felt renewed anguish over the losses she had experienced so long ago. Separated by distance, and limited by the time we could spend together, my mother and I found our vacations together a time to bond. In our travels together, her hearing loss made it difficult to converse together, especially in public places where her loudness would render me self-conscious, although it did not bother her in the least. To pass the time, I often urged her to recall memories of her past. Since her hearing was so poor, I listened to her stories and recorded them. As I recorded, she spoke more fluently; both she and I felt her oral history would be for posterity—for our children and family.

This was different from my siblings who, in their frustrations, argued and yelled. They were always trying to get her to hear what they wanted her to hear. The more they yelled, the less she heard. I merely listened to what she wanted to say. I heard the wisdom and continuity of her simple words. She had been educated only up until the 6th grade, which was average for girls in her time, but is limited by today's standards. Knowing this, and modest about her peasant background, she was reticent to talk at first. But spurred by my interest and her wish to transmit and preserve our family history, she recounted and shared her view of the world. I recorded these memories for her, for us, for history.

My mother's story is a saga of contrasts, of immigration, of culture, and of poverty. Through her eyes, this saga speaks of intergenerational bonds, of mothers and daughters, and of survival and striving. It records what my mother believed, in her modesty and simplicity, to be too mundane and insignificant to be recorded. And yet it is her voice that I hear, that calls to me, to remind me of her wisdom and of the limitless boundaries of the world today. It speaks to the impact of immigration, of poverty, and of the sociopolitical context on the lives of immigrant families. This saga is told in her voice.

MEMORIES OF CHINA: THE JOURNEY

My mother was 70 when I began this recording of her oral history, which continued until her death at the age of 84 in 1994. She would have been 94 today, almost a century from the beginning of her experience. The themes in her story are relevant to the struggle of all immigrants as they make their journey.[1]

The Sojourner [1890–1910]

The California gold rush initiated the large immigration of Chinese to America. Many of the young men in Toisan went to *gnoy yerng* [overseas] to find their fortune. *Gnoy yerng,* that's what we called America. You never had to worry about having something to eat. Everyone was rich there. How we envied all those young men who would bring back gold and riches for their families.

Ah Gung [Maternal Grandfather], your grandfather, my father, was no different. There were no opportunities left in Toisan. All we could do was farm; yet the land was barren. The floods were frequent, washing out the rice fields from time to time. There was often nothing to eat since we depended on the land. People were dying. Beggars filled the streets. America beckoned to all of us. This was our hope. The passage from China to America took one month by boat; there was no plane travel in those days. People would get seasick since most had never even sat on a train or in a car. They would get dizzy and were unable to eat for the whole month waiting to get to America.

Ah Gung had saved barely enough money to make the passage; he was determined to become prosperous for our sake. People really did not know where they would end up, only that they were going to *gnoy yerng*. It was America; it was the Golden Mountain. Ah Gung ended up in Vancouver working for the *lo faan* ["Mr. Foreigner," or whites] in the gold mines. *Lo faan,* that's what we call white people. Chinese were not allowed to mine gold in those days, only to work for the gold miners. Chinese were not allowed any real status. We could only get the jobs nobody wanted. Once in America, we struggled to make ends meet. Sometimes the suffering was as bad as it was in Toisan. This was true for Ah Gung when he got to America, only we did not know it at the time.

The letters we got never said a word. Ah Gung was a proud man; he would never write to tell us how difficult it was or how hard he worked. Only when he returned to China did we learn how hard it had been; there were times when he did not know from where his next meal would come. When he realized the opportunities in the gold mines were reserved only for white people, he tried his luck elsewhere. He was determined not to give up. He tried to open a restaurant but that failed after one year. Then, he opened a grocery store but that also failed.

Very little is known about what happened since Ah Gung was not one to tell us too much. We had to guess and piece together from the few things he would say. When he returned to China, he brought home gold dust worth about $800, not much even in those days. But he was a proud man; I never dared complain that this was all he had to show for the ten years he spent away from home. Ah Gung was a good father; he provided for the family. He was the Sojourner.

The Good Brother: Family Obligation

I lost my mother when I was 5.[2] Poy Q's [Maternal Uncle Poy][3] parents took Dai Q [Eldest Maternal Uncle][4] and me in. Dai Q was 15 and I was 5 at the time. Without my parents around, I had no one to protect me from the meanness of the other children. Poverty does strange things to people; people look down on you. Not having a mother, I was *dern* [pitiful]. I would eye the other children enviously as their mothers would fend for them and hoard the best food for them. I would always talk about Ah Gung proudly to my friends to prove to them that I too had a parent who cared. I would say, "My father is in *gnoy yerng,* and is taking good care of us." He always sent money home so Poy Q's parents would take good care of me. Along with it was always a letter telling us about what he was doing. From his letters, I imagined that the streets in America were paved with gold. I imagined that he was living the life of an emperor with servants at his beckon serving his every need. Privately, I cried myself to sleep many a night over not having a mother to watch over me. Little did I imagine how much Ah Gung had suffered. It was not until his later years back in China that he would lament, "Going out into the world to find one's fortune is a fate more pitiful than the life of a dog."[5] Ah Gung [Maternal Grandfather] was a good brother, my mother would say. To repay Poy Q's father for taking care of me, he tried to help him get a new start; he gave his brother money to start a business. Besides, this was a must since Ah Gung was the eldest son in the family. His advice to Poy Q was "Don't rely on people. You must work hard to make your own living. This way, you'll always be independent." Poy Q always remembers these words of advice and tells me so to this day. Poy Q went on to start his business as a shirtmaker in Hong Kong. We always had this bond since we grew up together in the same household. Although we are first cousins, we are as close as any sister and brother. That's why I helped him to immigrate here to America.[6]

Unfortunately, Poy Q's father was not so lucky. He "bought papers" twice trying to emigrate out of China.[7] The first "paper" expired because Poy Q's father needed to get surgery for his *sa-gnon* ["sandy eye"].[8] The second "paper" Poy Q's father bought limited his entry to Canada; he never made it there either. Ah Gung then gave money to Poy Q's father to help him emigrate to France. He felt it was Poy Q's father's turn now to go out in the world to find his fortune. First, Ah Gung gave him $500; later, he gave him another $300. That was a lot of money in those days. But Poy Q's father could not find a job in France; things are never as easy as our imagination would have us think. He could not make a go of it. Ah Gung finally sent money to Poy Q's father to help him return home to marry in China.

Ah Gung was a good man. He did all these things not expecting to be repaid; he just wanted to be appreciated. That is a virtue in our culture. That is why Poy Q treats me so good now; he is repaying his father's debt. He is very respectful; he always remembers. Poy Q will often come up to visit me and take me out for dim sum even though I don't eat very much. It is the gesture that counts. He never forgets my birthday; he always brings a chicken to honor me.

The Irrevocable Losses [1911–1930]

I was the fifth and youngest of five children. Three of my siblings died; my sister died when she was seven. I had two brothers who died; one died when he was eight; the other when he was ten. That left just me and Dai Q, who was ten years older than me. Times were tough during those days in China. When people got sick, there was not the medicine to do anything about it. Many times, we did not even know what they died of. That's why we had so many rituals to protect us just in case there were evil spirits around wishing us ill will. On the other hand, maybe it is all in one's fate; a person's life is destined to follow a certain course. You can't change fate; you just have to accept it.

I was born July 23 in *Men-Guo* Year One [1911][9] in Hoiping, China in the village of Hen Gong. This is a village in the Canton province, not far from Toisan where your father was born. People stayed in their villages for life. That's why families "take in a daughter-in-law." When a woman leaves her village upon marriage, she lives in her husband's village for the rest of her life even if he dies. She belongs to her husband's family.

When I was born, I was named Gim Slen [New Gold]. When Gim Nul [Golden Daughter] my older sister died, I was renamed Tel Hai because my mother was afraid I too would die. They thought the old names were now bad omens. Hai means another younger brother will come soon. My parents were trying to change fate by renaming me; the words of my name are symbols of bringing new life. But I never liked this name because I lost my mother under this name. So when I turned 13, I took the name of Mei Yee [Beautiful Start]. Ah Gung, your grandfather, had returned from *gnoy yerng* by then, and I wanted a new start.

Ah Gung was 20 years old when Dai Q, my brother, was born. He was 30 years old and gold mining in Vancouver, Canada when I was born. By the time I was 5, I had no mother anymore. In July of that same year, Ah Gung's mother, my grandmother, died. So I lost both my mother and grandmother when I was 5. Ah Gung wanted to make sure there was someone to take care of me. He wrote to Poy Q's father to ask him this favor. With the money from Ah Gung, Poy Q's father was now in a position to marry. He quickly married Cherng Por [Great Maternal Aunt] so that she could help Ah Gung raise me. These events were described in a matter of fact manner because it was so commonplace in China. There was little choice in the affairs of marriage since decisions are left to elders, parents, and matchmakers.

Cherng Por resented being forced to raise me; she felt like a stepmother even though she was only my aunt. Poor her, I can't blame her! She was only 16 years old at the time she was forced to marry Poy Q's father. So she took it out on me; she was mean and treated me very poorly. Sometimes, I would fall asleep on the floor because I had no mother to put me to bed. She would just leave me there; I was so *dern* [pitiful]. Yet Cherng Por would dote on and spoil her own children, Poy Q and his sister. She carried Poy Q on her back until he was 3 while I had to fend for myself. Like my mother, Cherng Por had 6 children, three of whom died before Poy Q was born. I've forgiven her now; I honor her now that she is here in the United States.

The Reunion: Father–Daughter Bonds

In *Men-Guo* 13 [1924], Ah Gung returned to China from Vancouver. He was 43 now and had been away for 13 years. I was 13 when he remarried that September. Dai Q was 23; he also married in November of that same year. This was the best and worst years of my life. I was still living in Hoiping when news arrived of Ah Gung's return home. On January 2, Men-Guo 14 [1925] when I turned 14, I was told to accompany Dai Q and Dai Kim [Eldest Maternal Aunt], his new wife, and Ah Por [Maternal Grandmother], my new stepmother, to join Ah Gung in Nanjing. I had never left the village before this, and Nanjing was cold. I was thrilled that my father was coming home. I would now have someone to care for me.

The journey to Nanjing was long and hard. We lived in the city of Guangzhou for a few days, and then traveled for 7 days by boat to Shanghai. Ah Gung came out to Shanghai to pick us up at the designated meeting place. I was anxious and so excited. I had only seen him in pictures; I did not recognize him at first. When he arrived, I waited for Dai Q to introduce us; this was only proper since he was the elder brother. We politely acknowledged one another. We proceeded on our journey together. We all stayed in a hotel for two nights, and then traveled for 4 hours from Shanghai to Nanjing. Next, we rode a "taxi" to Bonkei, a suburb of Nanjing where we were to live.

This reunion of father and daughter was a defining moment embedded in my mother's memory. Every minute detail of the days preceding her reunion with Ah Gung was remembered; each moment was savored as a precious gem. This reunion at the vulnerable age of 13 was the culmination of years of pent-up feelings since losing her mother at age 5. It demonstrated her father's concern for her welfare, his remembering her, and his keeping his promise to return and reunite the family after 13 years. Her father was a hero and protector, perhaps all the more necessary to counter her feelings of shame, anger, and loss of her mother at so young an age.

Upon arrival to Nanjing, Ah Gung set about to build a house for his new wife. Alas, this marriage was short-lived. You see, my potential step-mother had a 7-year-old daughter from a previous marriage whom she had brought with her to this marriage. This did not fit with Ah Gung's plan. He was concerned for our welfare. His intent to remarry was to reunite the family; he also had not told her that he was planning to return to Canada shortly. When the new wife found out his plan, she refused to stay in Nanjing alone and ended the marriage. She returned the gold bracelets from the dowry to Ah Gung to compensate for the cost of the wedding banquet and expenses. Everyone was so poor in those days that this was considered only fair.

Ah Gung then went about to look for another wife because he wanted me to have a mother. Through a matchmaker, he finally remar-ried. Ah Nerng [Stepmother] was over 30 with two children from a pre-vious marriage; her husband had been an opium addict. She did not have too many options; few men in those days were interested in women with this kind of history; they were considered tainted and immoral. Ah Gung refused to allow Ah Nerng to bring the two children [age 7 and 3] with her into our home because of me; he was always concerned for my welfare.[10] Ah Nerng's former mother-in-law was angry when she found out about the marriage because she had expected Ah Nerng to remain in her household according to Chinese custom. Ah Nerng's former mother-in-law came looking for retribution. She hid while Poy Q paid her off with about $20 to get her to leave our house. Ah Gung and Ah Nerng had one daughter from this marriage; Ah Yee [Maternal Aunt], named Gim Hing [Golden Sibling] is 13 years younger than me, and still lives in Nanjing.

Ah Gung later returned to Canada once again to find his fortune, leaving me in the care of Ah Nerng. She was mean. She played favorites, giving her own child Ah Yee everything. I was resentful and jealous of her. When I would ask Ah Nerng for money to buy books, she would go straight to Ah Gung to complain; he would then scold me for being so greedy. You see, girls are not supposed to be greedy; if you ask for some-thing, you are considered greedy. So Ah Nerng always knew how to manipulate the situation against me. Ah Yee always got the better of things; I got the leftovers. When I couldn't take it anymore, I cried to Ah Gung one day, saying, "I didn't think not having a mother would be so *dern* [pitiful]." We then cried together commiserating over losing my mother. I always hated Ah Yee because I felt jealous of all the attention she got from Ah Nerng. She really is all right though. We write to each other now all the time.

Ah Nerng wanted to arrange to marry me off when I was only 14 so that she would be rid of me. Ah Gung refused because of his concern for me. He said it would be *dern* to marry me off so young. He accused Ah Nerng of being *too-sum* [heartless]. He insisted that she raise me until at least age 18 or 19 before marriage. Ah Gung then asked the next door neighbor, Ah Seem [Auntie][11] to watch over me. Ah Gung made her promise to arrange a marriage only when I became of marrying age and to help find a good man for me. He had the utmost concern for me.

PREPARING FOR AMERICA

The First Meeting: Husband and Wife

In *Men-Kuo* 17 [1928], Papa [my father] came from *gnoy yerng* [overseas] to Nanjing to find a wife. Our neighbor, Ah Sook [Uncle] met him one day and asked him if he was married. He told Papa that there was this Wong girl living next door to him who might be eligible for marriage; he was talking about me. He then told Papa, "Let me ask if she is willing. When she gets out of school, she always walks by and calls out to me. She is a good girl. She walks by here everyday; you can take a look for yourself." Papa then watched for me through this neighbor's window. When I walked by, he said OK, he was willing to marry me although he thought I was kind of small for my age; I am barely 4'10". Important characteristics for a good marriage in China were that a woman be of good moral character and a man be able to support a family. Papa and I were then formally introduced. We did not talk when we first met; I was shy and modest. Papa approved of this because he felt good girls should be shy. Ah Seem, the neighbor, gave me her opinion about Papa. She said he looked *loh-seet* [honest] and *deung-tom* [smart], but was concerned because he had a *pei-hay* [temper]. [My mother smiled, saying Ah Seem was very *gnon-tom*— had a sharp eye—for predicting Papa's character.] When I first saw Papa, I neither liked nor disliked him; there is no such thing as love at first sight; all marriages were arranged. Whatever the elders said was okay with me; I was very obedient. Besides, Ah Nerng was not good; she was mean to me.

I felt I needed a *mon-how* [entrance or home] to go to. I was 17 years old by then and of marrying age. I cried that whole night because I felt I had no choice. It was a long and lonely night. I knew it was time to get married. I knew I would have to accept what the elders had decided. My fate had been decided, and I couldn't look back.

Papa and I became engaged August 4, *Men-Guo* 17 [1928]; we married on August 24, *Men-Guo* 17 [1928] when I was 17 years old. After we were married a month, I was *y yeen* [with child]. Papa had built a new house in Nanjing for the family. We lived there together after the marriage for a year and 4 months. Papa then left again to go *gnoy yerng* [overseas]. As my father and uncle had done, I knew this was the way things were to be. I did not protest. Papa returned to Mexico on January 2, *Men-Guo* 19 [1930]; I was 19 then and did not see him again for the next 9 years when I was 28 [1939]. I tried to be patient and pass the time while I waited. I knew he would return and would not abandon me.

The Omen: The First Born

Did you know you had a brother who died?[12] I gave birth to Kok Nong, my first son, on August 6, *Men-Guo* 18 [1929]; he died August 21, *Men-Guo* 19 [1930] when he was only 1. Circumstances around his death were very strange indeed. He had not been sick. On that particular day, I had brought some food to a neighbor, leaving him home. By the time I returned home, I found that he had fallen on the floor as if he was sick. We brought him to a Chinese doctor who said he was not ill but could not tell us what was wrong. I did not know what to do and wanted to put him in the hospital. I was persuaded by neighbors not to because they were afraid he would die there. I should not have listened because he died 16 days later. Hospitals are bad omens; people die there.

After the fall, Kok Nong was fine during the day; but in the evening, he would cry all night as if the *gul* [demons] were disturbing him. I felt the *gul* caused him to die because he had not been sick. I then consulted a *seen doctor* [soothsayer] about him. The soothsayer prophesized that "Sitting in front of a door facing East, he met up with two *gul-seen* [demon spirits], a male and female spirit; the female was carrying the baby on her back." I tried to figure out what this meant. Our house sat with the front door facing East so this prophecy must have been referring to our house.

In fact, I had had a dream recently in which I saw two people I knew coming down by our house. Both these people had committed suicide so I knew this omen could not be a good one. One of these people was a Lee woman who had hung herself because her mother-in-law was no good and so terrible to her. In the dream, this woman said to me, "Tel, your child is so cute," and tried to reach out to touch him. Kok Nong started to cry in the dream. I awoke in a start and found him actually crying. I knew I had been carrying him sitting at the front door with several friends enjoying the breeze. This had to be a bad omen. The soothsayer also predicted that the baby would have only three more lives [meaning three more days left to live].

I found out later that at about the same time all this was happening, Papa had gone hunting in America and shot a goose. His friends had warned him not to do this since it was considered bad luck to kill a goose. Papa pooh-poohed their warnings saying he was not afraid. He always had a lot of guts. Kok Nong's death was probably retribution for what Papa did.[13]

The circumstances occurring up to Kok Nong's death were really strange; he was never really sick. After he fell, Kok Nong behaved very strangely, as if he was possessed. He would eat, but had no bowel movements. We watched over him for 16 days. On his last day, he tried to reach for me and called out "Mama." I wanted so much to go to him. But the old women, the elders in the neighborhood who had gathered around, ordered me to my bedroom; they told me not to answer him. They said the look in his eyes was not good. They were trying to prevent Kok Nong from dying; they believed that he would not leave to go to the next world if I, his mother, would not respond to his cry. I was in agony. I left the room as I was told, hoping he would pull through, but he died anyway. I remember him fondly; he was very smart. He was barely one and could do so much. When he saw people approaching, he would point them out to me. Do you know that he looked like you?

The Long Wait [1930-1939]: Lau and Lee Clans

The wait for Papa was long. I tried to pass the time. World War II was soon to come. The Japanese had already begun to invade China. With these change of events, Papa decided that China was unsafe, and began to make plans for me to join him in America. I continued living alone in Nanjing until your Lau Ah Year [Lau Paternal Grandfather] invited me to visit GuangZhou village when I was 21. He was trying to use me as a pawn to get Papa to return to the Lau family.

Papa was born a Lau and adopted by the Lees. As the story goes, Lau Ah Yeen [Paternal Grandmother] was collecting *chai* [firewood] while she was pregnant with Papa. The stress from this induced premature labor. Lau Ah Yeen died during childbirth. Papa was the third of three sons who were 6 years old and 3 years old at the time. Papa came from a well-educated family and pedigreed background. Lau Ah Year was a teacher. The eldest son was later educated at Wong Poo Military Academy, a very reputable school in Toisan.

Papa was considered unlucky by the Lau clan since his birth caused his mother's death. The Laus wanted to rid themselves of this fate. They already had two sons. When he was only 7 days old, Lau Ah Year wrapped Papa up and abandoned him. The Lee clan from a nearby village heard of this situation in the Lau clan; news spreads quickly. The Lees had three daughters, one of whom died recently at birth. Since everyone wants boys, the Lee clan decided to adopt Papa and bring him home so that he would receive the milk of Lee Ah Yeen [Lee Paternal Grandmother] who was still nursing. The Lees planned to raise Dad as a replacement for the baby who died. When Papa was taken in, it was obvious he had been neglected; he was unwashed and had been soaking in his own feces for some time.

In the Lee family, Papa's fate was changed; he was the favored child. He was spoiled rotten and honored because his entrance had changed the luck in the family. Two sons were born to Lee Ah Yeen after Papa entered the Lee clan. When Papa reached adulthood, Lau Ah Year had a change of heart. He regretted having given up your Papa for adoption. He now tried to get Papa to return to the Lau clan and to recognize him as father. Papa refused out of loyalty to his adoptive parents to whom he always remained indebted for raising him. However, he later agreed to call Lau Ah Year his godfather to acknowledge these biological ties. This did not stop Lau Ah Year from continuing to try to bribe Papa with gifts to win his affection and maintain the family lineage. In later years, Lau Ah Year would often invite Papa to the Lau clan celebrations. It was Lau Ah Year who gave Papa those 9 gold coins that he brought with him to the America. These were the coins I gave to you as a teenager; you were careless in losing them when you brought them to the jeweler; there was nothing I could do to get them back because I can't speak English.[14]

I never thought much of your Lau Ah Year. I felt he was manipulative. On the other hand, the Lee clan was more virtuous. Lee Bahk Gung [Paternal Great Grandfather] was also a sojourner. He left for *gnoy yerng* one month after his marriage. He lived in San Francisco working on the railroads. He returned to China decades later at the age of 61. He felt he had achieved his goal because he was able to buy 40 acres of land for the family. Lee Bahk Por [Paternal Great Grandmother] was 50 by the time he came home; consequently, there were no children from this union. Lee Bahk Por was angry with him because she felt her life had gone by. She chided him, "If you were home, we would have had a houseful of children by now, and there would be people to work on the farm. Now we're old and there is nothing."

Lee Ah Bahk Gung, on the other hand, felt there was no future in the village; he came back only for his retirement. This was typical of many of the early Chinese sojourners. He advised Papa to "Always carry $50 for security. Go live elsewhere. Don't come back to the village." His advice was instrumental to Papa's future; this is why he too went to *gnoy yeung*. When he was ready to seek a wife, he went to Nanjing and found me. That's how fate brought us together.

Because there were no children from the Lee great-grandparents, your Lee Ah Year [Paternal Grandfather] was adopted along with his sister. Lee Ah Year did not like to work. Life was hard in the village so he decided to immigrate to Hawaii in 1910 when Papa was 6 years old. As I told you before, Papa had two older sisters. One was married. The other died a year after her marriage; she committed suicide because she was so unhappy in the marriage. Women didn't have choices in those days if their in-laws were no good. Suicide was often the only escape.

As I told you, Papa's entrance into the Lee clan brought two younger brothers, Ben Khin, your Sam Suk [Number Three Paternal Uncle], and Fook Ho, your Yee Suk [Number Two Paternal Uncle]. He was originally named Ben Ho, following Papa's name of Ben On. Shortly after he was born, however, someone by the same name in the village died so they changed his name to change his fate.

During the Japanese war in China, all your uncles and their families died of starvation. Sam Suk had a wife and two sons; they died during World War II from starvation. Yee Suk went to tend the buffalo; he was lucky because this meant he had a job, which provided him with food to eat for a while. The Lee clan did not own any farmland so there was no food to eat when times got tough. This was particularly true during wartimes or drought seasons. Yee Suk died 2 years ago. He had a second wife and two children; they all also died of starvation. Of the nine from the Lee clan, only the eldest son of Sam Suk named Ah Keung survived; he is still living in Toisan village. We sent him money to get married some time ago; he has one son and three daughters. I also sent money to his children, my great nephews, for them to get married. They asked for $600; I only sent $200 each. They are always asking for money. That was all I could afford since I am on Social Security; but the money goes a long way back in China. I don't know what happened to them now. [15]

A Man's Character

Papa had a bad temper but a kind heart. He was not afraid to die; he would fight with his life and confront any situation head-on. You remember when he would not let any of the laundry customers *ha-ba* [intimidate] him. He would risk his life before he would let the *lo faan* [foreigners or whites] intimidate him. This was foolish at times since he couldn't escape being in the laundry, but he protected us. That's how he survived the racism here in America.

He was defiant even as a child. There was a Hong Ah Bahk [Village Uncle][16] who was financially well off, but arrogant. You had to worry about these people in those days because they liked to push their weight around. He tried to *ha-ba* [intimidate] Papa by belittling him, thinking Papa would be afraid of him. Papa fought with him instead. He went into this guy's house, took his wok, and threw it on the floor to insult him. That was gutsy. He then stomped on and killed his chickens; you know how people treasured their means for food. Lee Ah Yeen was bearing Sam Suk at the time; Lee Ah Year had already died so she was already overburdened. When this Hong Ah Bahk came to complain about Papa's behavior, Lee Ah Yeen was so distraught, she beat Papa with a stick. Papa felt this was unjust; so he grabbed the stick used to stir the *geesee gon* [pigsty] and hit her back. Papa claims this was the only time Lee Ah Yeen had ever hit him.[17] Papa was always proud of how fresh and defiant he was as a child, even toward his mother. You remember how he used to proudly describe the time he was punished by being hung by his legs and arms from a tree. He was so stubborn that even this could not sway him; he refused to repent at all costs.

Since Lee Ah Year was in *gnoy yerng,* other Hong Ah Bahk [Village Uncles] would try to help Lee Ah Yeen raise Papa. They would watch over Papa, trying to teach him and provide him with male role models.

It's always difficult when your father is not around to teach you. Another Hong Ah Bahk gave money for Papa to study kung fu. He thought this would help to discipline him; Papa stopped misbehaving after this. In fact, he was Moi Goo's [Younger Paternal Aunt][18] father who we used to visit regularly. Did you know that she was well educated in China?—It's a tragic story. She was brilliant and well known for her scholarly calligraphy. Here in America, she was a laundrywoman like everyone else. She never could accept this fate, and tried unsuccessfully to start other businesses here. Her husband, Ah Cherng [Husband of Younger Paternal Aunt], did not support or understand her. She became frustrated and depressed; she got more forgetful, would get lost in her daydreams, and then neglect her family and work.

By the way, Moi-Goo's father was a big, wealthy lawyer who trained in Beijing. Did you know that he was murdered by an angry client who knew how to *em-mak* [acupressure]? He had four *tep-see* [concubines]; in those days, wealthy men had many *tep-see* to demonstrate their social status. Moi Goo was from the second mother while Set-Soon Dai-Goo [Set-Soon, Eldest of the Younger Paternal Aunts] was from the first mother. His fourth *tep-see* was given to him as a gift in payment for legal services to become his servant; she became his fourth concubine. Because there were no children from this marriage, she was forced to leave the family. Women were property, and bearing children was important to a wife's status and honor in those days. It was the only way to guarantee one's place in the family. A wife was shamed, and could not hold her head up, if she could not bear children—women's bondage. People were poor, and there were no choices.

Yee-Moon Suk was another Lee Hong Ah Sook [Village Younger Uncle] who ended up in New York City. We used to visit him regularly as well. He had a reputation for siding with the winning side whichever it was—described as *tul-fung-by* [blows with the wind] by those who knew him. He lacked integrity. He sided with the Japanese when they invaded and occupied China. Later, when the communists overruled China, he switched sides again. Character is important to a man. One must stand up to one's beliefs even if it means suffering the consequences.

A Woman's Virtue

I visited Toisan village in Guangzhou when I was 21 at the beckoning of your Lau Ah Year. I had nothing to do; I was biding my time while I waited for your Papa to return. It was already 4 years. The return to Toisan village was an unpleasant experience so I was anxious to return to Nanjing after a year; I was 22 by then. While I was in Toisan, your Lau Ah Year wrote a letter to Papa telling him that I was frivolous. He was trying to force me to stay in the village so he could always reach Papa for money. I was furious with him for trying to tarnish my character by attacking my virtue; I have not forgiven him to this day.[19]

This caused trouble between Papa and me because good women are not supposed to be frivolous; it is a sign of bad character to be wanting excitement and spending money. Lau Ah Year's letter declared that I was *moe-sam goo-ga* [lacking interest in tending to the family]. Papa was concerned that I lacked character and wrote to Yee Bahk [Number Two Elder Paternal Uncle]. Yee Bahk tried to help; he brought the letter to Lau Ah Year and confronted him. In trying to support me, he defied his father and ended up in an argument with him. Lau Ah Year was angry at this accusation by his own son; he smacked him for being so disrespectful. Do you know what Lau Ah Year then did? He took away all the money Papa had sent to me to prevent me from leaving Guangzhou. I felt imprisoned and trapped in Guangzhou. I was worried that I would never be able to get out of the Toisan village.

In desperation, I wrote to Papa and appealed to him to send money to Dai Q to help me leave. I wrote to Dai Q to ask for his help; I asked him to come get me, and take me back to Bonkei, Nanjing. I finally was able to leave. When I returned to Nanjing, I decided to resume school because I had nothing to do. I was still waiting for your Papa; I finished grade 6.

The Adoption

When I was 23, I adopted Sel Ming, your brother; he was 7 months old, born in October or November. His mother had been a poor farmer. The family had nothing to eat except a few morsels of bread and *jook* [congee]. He was so pitiful when I first took him in. His clothes were all patched and worn; even the patches were patched. Sel Ming's mother needed money for food to feed the rest of the family so they would not starve. She decided to sell Sel Ming since he was the third child. This was common practice then; it was your only choice when you were poor. No one wanted him because he was so small; they figured he was unhealthy. She asked me to adopt him, begging on her knees for me to take Sel Ming as his chance for survival. She bared her breast to me to show how her nipples had been bitten sore from nursing because she had no milk. She cried profusely and was so desperate she was even going to just leave Sel Ming there. All the relatives urged me to take him; they took pity on her. The poor woman was asking $40 for him. When we finally agreed to the deal, the broker took $20 for his expenses, leaving the poor woman with only $20 for herself. I took pity on her as she cried and gave her an extra $20.

For the next five years, Sel Ming and I lived in Nanjing, waiting to hear from your Papa. It was nice to be raising a child again. It kept me busy, and we spent some pleasant times together. I preferred this less rigid city life in Nanjing to the small-mindedness of the Toisan vlllage. World World II and communism was soon to change this pace of waiting and watching the passing of life.

The Escape from Nanjing [1937]

Then World War II started. It was a nasty war. The Japanese invaded Shanghai on July 7, *Men-Guo* 26 [1937], and were headed for Nanjing. When the news broke, we were afraid. We prepared to flee our homes and head for Hong Kong. We rushed to escape since we heard stories of atrocities committed by the Japanese soldiers; civilians, including women and children, were tortured and killed, leaving no survivors. There were stories of women first being raped, and then slit with a sword right up the middle. This was a most difficult and traumatic time for me. From Nanjing, we had to reach a boat in Guangzhou in order to make the passage to Hong Kong. This was over 1,000 miles; transportation was poor in those days. The whole city was in chaos; there were people fleeing from all over. Some people walked for 7 days straight to get there and were exhausted. Others, not used to the city, had come down from the mountains and were bewildered.

We fled Nanjing by train to get to Guangzhou. I was carrying Sel Ming on my back. I carried only one bag with a change of underwear; we had to leave most of our belongings because we could not carry them. First, we rode a fire-car [train] for two whole days from Nanjing to Mowu. Our whole family left together, including Dai Q, Sel Ming, Ah Gung, Ah Por, Poy Q, and Hing Q. For 3 days and nights, we rode the train. The train was packed with standing room only. There was no place to sit; there was no place to move. We had to sleep standing up. It was a long and strenuous trip. I carried Sel Ming on my back during this entire trip. I was exhausted and weak. After 2 days of riding like this, a soldier sitting in front of me took pity on me and told me to sit on his lap. There was no place to move or he would have given me his seat. He assured me not to worry about his intentions and insisted that I sit. I finally complied [not worrying about improprieties] because I was so tired.

There was no food or toilets on the train. All I had with me for food was a thermos of water and some soda crackers; that did not last very long. Everyone did his or her daily functions standing up; there was no place to go. We all tolerated the stench from one another. Several women were in the advanced stages of pregnancy. When they were due to deliver, the people standing nearby tried to move aside to make some room. The poor women had to give birth standing up. As for me, I began menstruating at some point during the trip; I was unable to change or clean myself up; I was soaked in blood. I was embarrassed but you can't think about it during times like that. We were all exhausted. But we dared not complain; we were frightened that the Japanese would overtake us and just felt lucky enough to be able to escape.

The train stopped at Cherng Sa for a rest. People were afraid to get off the train for fear that they could not get back on. Local residents came to the side of the train to sell us rice. Most of us hungrily grabbed for these limited morsels since we had not eaten for 2 days. One person had not finished eating when the train began to leave the station. The lady who sold the rice became frantic wanting to get her bowl back. Being poor, she was afraid she would be out a bowl. Others on the train took pity on her. Finally, someone threw some money out of the window as the train was pulling away to pay for the bowl.

We were finally able to rest at Nam Hung after traveling for 4 days before starting out again on a boat for Hong Kong. It was crowded at the pier where the boat was docked. Everyone was frantic and anxious; they were afraid they would not get on. We waited on the pier all day from 6 p.m. to 6 a.m. the next morning so as not to lose our place in line. There was only one gangway and a mass of humanity struggling to reach safety. Everyone was fighting to board the boat; we had to use each other as a human ladder to get onboard. We climbed up from the pier through a porthole because we could not reach the gangway.

There were 30 of us who fled from Nanjing together, including Poy Q, Hing Q, Dai Q and his family, Ah Gung, Ah Por, the Yeps and the Louies. Again the boat was packed. Seven of us had to sleep on one bed. There was no place to sit. We had to stand all night again until the boat arrived in Horn How. That's why those of us who made it to America are so close. [20]

Those of us from Nanjing were on the first boat out of Nam Hung. When the boat returned to pick up a second load of passengers, it was bombed and destroyed by the Japanese. There were no survivors. News was slow and not always accurate during those days. News reached America that a boat had been bombed. Not knowing that there were two boats, Papa thought I had been killed. He moaned that "all was lost" and was in despair until he received my letter several weeks later that I was safe in Hong Kong. Once in Hong Kong, we heard that the Japanese invaded Nanjing the day after we left and had pillaged the village. We were thankful that we were lucky enough to escape in time. That's why I have such strong feelings against the Japanese to this day.[21]

◄ My mother and father in the living
room of our Brooklyn apartment
above the Hand Laundry.

My mother and father in a formal ►
portrait, one of the few ever
taken, given my father's
aversion to being
photographed.

▲ Second reunion of my mother
with my brother, Sel Ming, in Nanjing
China 42 years after they separated;
family bidding farewell to us at the train
station.

My mother with her nephews, me, ►
and my son Scott at the Temple of
Heaven in Beijing.

My father, mother, brother, sister, and me ▶
in Brooklyn, under the elevated trains
during a visit to my brother's godparents.

Ah Gung, my grandfather, taken in
China before 1937. ▼

Family reunion in Nanjing; I meet ▶
the Wong clan for the first time.

My mother and father in Plymouth,
MA after I moved to Boston. ▼

First family reunion and farewell of my ▶
mother and father with Sel Ming 33 years
after they separated.

My mother with
Sel Ming, together
in the United States
after 50 years. ▼

▲ My mother during a trip to Paris.

▲ Reunion in 1981 of my mother
and her half-sister Ah Yee (far left)
and my brother Sel Ming in Nanjing.

◄ My mother and her grandchildren
at my sister's 25th wedding
anniversary celebration.

Reunion of my mother with Sel Ming, ▶
42 years after they separated; I meet my
brother and his wife for the first time.

My mother at my sister's 25th
wedding anniversary. ▼

Mom with me and my sons ▶
in Hawaii in 1989.

◀ My mother's 80th birthday
celebration with all her children.

CHAPTER 5

Day by Day: Of Women and Culture

From a Child's View

I just want to let you know
I understand what you've been going through.
If I could change things to be where you are,
I would go any distance, no matter how far.

Today is just the present, so let's look forward to tomorrow,
And try to put aside for a moment, any sadness or sorrow.
As parents, you both mean the world to me.
My love is forever and will always be.

Tracey Lynette Ong

My mother would remember and retell countless stories to us, as did my father. Each time a story was retold, it was told as if it were the first time. As children, we were impatient and restless. We dismissed these as the musings of adults who lived in the past with nothing better to do. As children, we had better things to do; we wanted to play. As my mother told these stories, there was always pride mixed with reminiscing. She always seemed to be teaching us something. As adults, these stories took on new meaning as we saw them through her eyes—they marked her fate, told about her journey, and were attempts to heal. But the deep pain always remained, and she could not be consoled. My mother's voice continues.

AMERICA THE MELTING POT:
THE IMMIGRATION MYTH

We all wanted to come to America. The stories we heard sounded like paradise. We all expected so much. We expected the streets to be paved with gold. Our stomachs would be full. We would never go wanting. All we had to do was work. Little did we know how hard that was to be, and that we would all be working in a laundry. The hours would be long; the days endless. We would feel different in a land where differences are not supposed to matter. Little did we think how much we would miss what we left behind, and long for the beauty and culture and essence of China. Back in the village, we used to pick lychees and other fruit off the trees. Family was always nearby; we felt safe since our neighbors all watched over one another. The passage of the oceans between China and America separated and bonded us through the letters we wrote and the stories we told about the Golden Mountain of the West. Many were exaggerated and distorted to make the unbearable bearable and to preserve the connections we needed—we created these legends of fortune. Most important, we could not lose face (shame) and could not bring ourselves to describe the squalid conditions under which we lived here in America. We needed to have face (pride); we maintained our loyalty and obligations to family and continued to send money back home to our extended families in Toisan from the meager earnings of a laundry.

The Abandonment and the Promise (1939)

After arriving safely in Hong Kong, I stayed with Poy Q, Hing Q, and Dai Q's family and made plans to join Papa in America. He had promised he would send for me. It was now almost 10 years, but I knew he would not abandon me. Papa had to buy papers to get me into the country since Chinese were not legally allowed to immigrate here given the quotas and anti-Asian legislation in effect at the time. Papa had intended to return to China with a fortune as all the early Chinese immigrants before him did; but the war prevented that from happening now. The only papers he could find which would fit my description were that of a citizen's daughter; this meant that I could not be married or have a child. I was devastated when I found this out. I agonized over this because I knew it meant I would have to leave Sel Ming behind; he was only 5 at the time. I didn't know how to handle this so I took the advice of the elders and did not tell him.

But children know better. Sel Ming knew that I was planning to leave without him, and insisted, "I want to go with my mother to America. If they don't let me through, I will sneak under the turnstile." I didn't know what to say to him. I only knew I could not take him with me. I couldn't bring myself to tell him the truth. He would be staying with Dai Q. I didn't know when we would be together again. All I could do was to give him my last piece of motherly advice. So I told Sel Ming, "You be good. Stay with Dai Q, Dai Kim, and Ah Por. They will take care of you. When I get to America, I will bring you over." I never forgot my promise to Sel Ming. Papa and I argued over this; immigration laws changed; China and America changed. But we kept this hope alive that one day, we would be reunited. After Papa died the Family Reunification Act of 1965 made it possible. I asked Willie, your brother, to initiate legal proceedings to bring Sel Ming over.

When it was time for me to leave, it was the feeling of the elders that it was better for me not to say goodbye because Sel Ming would be too upset. I woke up early that day to get ready while he was still sleeping. I packed a bag; there was little of value to bring. I was amazed how little this was compared to the vastness of the people and memories I was leaving behind. When Sel Ming woke up, Hing Q took him out to play to distract him. I then stole out with Dai Q who brought me to the boat en route to America. No one could deal with the separation. I was later told that when Sel Ming returned from playing and found out that I was gone, he became frantic. He cried in desperation and ran to the pier trying to catch up with me. He was depressed for quite a while after that.

Dai Kim raised him for me just as Cherng Por raised me after I lost my mother and Ah Gung left for *gnoy yerng*. Sel Ming lived with Dai Q and his family in Hong Kong for several years until they returned to Shanghai after the end of World War II to open a shirtmaking business. Dai Q later opened a department store in Nanjing; he was not successful and lost a lot of money.

At this point my mother became pensive, as if reliving once again the separation and abandonment of her son. I knew she was thinking how pitiful it was for him to grow up without his parents there to protect him. The pain in my mother's face was evident, but it was a fate over which she had had no control. As a child, I remember her crying whenever she spoke of this, but I could never fathom the depth of her pain. She would never admit to her feelings of guilt because it would have meant she could have done something about it. And so, there were words that were never spoken as she and I bonded in our silence. With a shrug, she said, "Life goes in cycles"—what goes around, comes around."

Paper Relatives: The Immigrant (1939–1955)

I arrived in America on January 5, 1939, from Hong Kong. The trip by boat took 18 days. We docked at Vancouver, Canada. I had a brief reunion with Ah Gung there and went on to Montreal. When I saw my father, I addressed him, "Pa." He then acknowledged me. We then spent a little time together. We were formal and cordial although the years of anguish still stirred inside. We each needed to maintain our dignity. I was now a grown woman, and going on to start a new life. This was to be the last time I would ever see him.

From there, I took another boat to San Francisco where I was detained on Angel Island for 3 months. It was ironic; I arrived there on Lunar New Year's Eve, a time we would have been celebrating and dining with family had I been back in China. It was one of the most depressing 3 months of my life on Angel Island; it was like being in prison. We were locked in our rooms, and had no freedom while we waited to be released. One of the interpreters took pity on us and tried to cheer us up at this detention center; he brought us chicken to celebrate the new year. I was petrified during my whole time there. I was afraid I would never get out of there. Periodically, the immigration authorities would take one of us into a room for interrogation about minute details of our lives. They would ask questions like: Describe the room in which your father lived in China? Was the bed on the left or the right? All the questioning were attempts to poke holes in our stories and catch us. We were in a hostile environment and were all afraid we would be caught lying and deported. This was the irony of my first taste of freedom in America.

On May 1, 1939, I finally received permission to leave Angel Island, and went to meet Papa in Boston. This was the point of entry. I was so relieved. Since Papa and I weren't supposed to be married, we got married once again to follow Western custom. We stayed in Boston for a week as a pseudo-honeymoon. Oliver Finds, my "paper father" was there to be witness at the ceremony. We even had another Chinese wedding banquet of three tables. We wanted to follow all the proper ceremony. The *lo faan* [Mr. Foreigner] there wondered why we were treating this in so matter-of-fact manner, thinking we Chinese were just unemotional. They didn't realize we were already married and had a child together. [My mother was amused and accommodated the fuss made by the *lo faan* over this Western style "wedding," but it simply did not have the meaning of her "real" wedding in China.]

From Boston, I went with Papa to New York to work in the laundry. It was only now, 11 years after my marriage that I first began to know the man I married. I learned that Papa left China on January 12, 1919 to come to Mexico to work as a farmer when he was 17. Since it was illegal to work until age 18, he added a year to his age in order to get work. Papa returned to China when he was 26 and married me when he was 27. After he left me, he wrote regularly. He told me he was going to America from Mexico. Whenever he wrote, I imagined all sorts of things. It seemed so simple, like a storybook. I couldn't really understand the magnitude of the difficulties and the dangers he faced, or the extent of the poverty he endured until I got here.

He came illegally into America in *Men-Guo* 21 (1932) under the assumed identity of a Lau; the papers he bought also happened to be his birth surname. Prior to leaving Mexico, he was afraid he would not make it to America so he made preparations in case he failed. He sent me $500 to put in the bank for safekeeping. If he made it to America, he would send for me and this money was to be given to Dai Q to raise Sel Ming. If he was deported, the money was to be used for him to start a business when he returned to China. As fate would have it, he made it.

According to Papa, there was just a barbed wire separating America from Mexico. He entered through Mississippi lying under the boxcar of a truck to escape detection. The compartment was just small enough to fit a person; it had a cover on top like a coffin. It was a terrifying ordeal since he would have been shot if caught. There was another person traveling with him who died, apparently frightened to death. Papa was *dai om* [had a lot of gall]; he was not afraid of anything. There was a Lo Lee [Mr. Lee] who picked him up in a limousine on the America side. The passage into America cost a lot of money in those days.

After arriving in America, Papa had to go undercover and hid in the On Leong clan association for three days. We went through a lot of difficulty and danger to just get a decent living in those days. Papa worked for a while in San Francisco as a dishwasher. Forn Sook (Uncle Forn) was return-ing to China and had recommended Papa for a job in Woo Ming Doon, Nor Ga Lon [Wilmington, North Carolina] on a vegetable farm; he worked there for about 1 year until it closed. That was how we got jobs in those days, through introduction. Papa then came to New York in *Men-Guo* 22 (1933) because he heard that there were many Chinese there. Upon arrival, he found work in a laundry on Myrtle Avenue in Brooklyn; that was the only kind of work Chinese could do then. It was work no one else wanted. You have to smell the foul odors of people. You were treated with no respect by the customers.

Papa finally saved enough money to buy a laundry of his own for $300 on Marcy Avenue, Brooklyn. This was everyone's dream at the time, to have one's own business even if it was only a laundry. Times were tough then; it was during the Great Depression in America; the Japanese were at war with China in Shanghai. Papa ended up sleeping on an iron-ing board in the laundry because he was too poor to buy a bed. When there was no business, he had no food to eat. Even so, he would send money back twice a year to support me; $200 at end of the year; $100 at midyear. This was enough to take care of me since expenses are so much lower in China. Life was not easy working in a laundry; I never real-ized how difficult it was until I got here. Customers taunt and disrespect you because you are Chinese. You have to tolerate it because there are no other choices for us to make a living.

Since Papa came to America under the paper name of Lau, he con-nected with Cher Long Fong, the Lau clan association in New York City. They befriended him as a relative and helped him get started. These fam-ily associations were safe havens for newcomers and provided financial and other social services on an informal basis. Papa was grateful for this help, but was too proud to ask for continuing help; besides everyone else was going through the same. [We considered them family and like most immigrants, we visited the association weekly on our Sunday outings to Chinatown during my childhood.] But Papa, as you know, always wanted us to keep it a secret that we were still associated with the Lee clan. He was afraid that he would be viewed as disloyal.

Born in America: The Impossible Dream (1941–1944)

Papa and I toiled in the laundry on Marcy Avenue for several years. He always believed spirits lived there. He claimed that he often saw two children sitting and swinging their legs in the back room. Whenever he went back there, they would disappear. We ignored these spirits at first, not knowing if they were good or evil spirits. Soon I was pregnant; but I miscarried when I was 4 months pregnant; this was before Ah Gor [Elder Brother] was born. I remember well the day I miscarried; Papa was not there. I had been standing on my feet all day ironing and working too hard in the laundry. Papa was visiting Mong Hong Bahk (Uncle Mong Hong) and returned home late. My stomach had been hurting all day, but I felt I had to keep going because there was so much work to be done. When Papa got home, he called a doctor who examined me and gave me some medicine to prevent a miscarriage; I miscarried anyway. My legs began hurting so bad that I couldn't walk.

Ah Gor, your brother, was born 1941, the year of the snake, just as World War II broke out. These were trying times while we were still living in the Marcy Avenue laundry. He had to suffer more because he was the first born. We were so busy working we had little time for him. You and your sister were lucky; you did not ever have to sleep in a laundry. There were many strange happenings there. Ah Gor would wake in the middle of the night crying. Papa believed the spirits in the laundry were causing this; he decided to rent an apartment around the corner on Park Avenue to get away from them. Papa found that sometimes if you dropped a ticket on the floor, it would come to rest standing up. Papa believed a spirit was holding it up. Even when there was wind blowing on the ticket, it would not fall. It was *ho kay kow* [so strange indeed]! Sometimes we would lose a laundry ticket. Neither of us knew where it went; it would just disappear. Later, the ticket would show up again in the same place. Papa felt the spirit had hidden the ticket and returned it. Why? I don't know.

Papa had been warned of these strange stories by the previous owner. At first, he did not believe them until it happened to him. He would hear noises, which must have been because of those spirits. Spirits will haunt a place where there has been unrest from some experience during their lives, usually some kind of trauma or feeling of injustice. We could never figure out who this spirit was.

Ah Jeer [Elder Sister] was born in 1942, the year of the Horse and just after World War II broke out. Ah Jeer is the caring one; she is always so thoughtful. I remember her watching me stir the coals and ashes of the heating stove in our Marcy Avenue apartment. My face was black from the ashes; my brow sweaty from the effort. I'll never forget what she told me. She said she would hire me a servant when she grows up so I would not have to work so hard. This was enough to sustain my energy for years to come.

You were born 1944, the year of the Monkey, as the war was coming to an end. You were born in the evening at 12:45 a.m. at Columbus Hospital, a Catholic hospital. You were all Catholic. The nuns there were very nice. I did not want the pregnancy because life in America was so difficult. While I was pregnant with you, I would have Ah Jeer bounce on my stomach to try to initiate a miscarrriage. I fear that was responsible for the birth defect on your lip. We went through years of surgery and huge medical bills; your health was weak. This must have been my punishment.

We lived in a poor area and did the best we could. When you were 1 year old, you were crying terribly one night in your crib. Papa was furious at having his sleep disturbed; you know how bad his temper was. He also could never forgive you for those huge medical bills; you know how he was about money. I was worried because of the threats he was making and tried to calm you down, thinking you were just being temperamental. It was not until morning that we discovered that a rat had bitten your thumb and there was blood all over the crib. We felt terrible then. You still have the scar to show for it.

Ah Gung died February 1950 in Nanjing from an earache; he was in his 70s. This was very sad for me; I was not able to be there when he died. I was told that he was not feeling well and went to sleep. In his sleep, he fell off the bed. Dai Kim was making *jook* [congee] for him when the grandchildren went in and found him. He had been in a good disposition the night before so I don't know why it happened. Ah Por had died earlier that year. I used to get earaches; I fear my hearing loss is hereditary. When you were young, Papa used a home remedy trying to heal my earache; this caused my permanent hearing loss. He was *dai om* [bold or audacious]; he heard vinegar was a remedy for earaches and poured it down my ear one day; I felt a shiver and lost the hearing in my left ear after that.

I sometimes blame Boon Moo [Paternal Elder Aunt Boon] for this. Shortly before Ah Gung's death, we had attended a funeral together. Upon returning from the cemetery, Boon Moo called me to look back at something. It is bad luck to look back when leaving a cemetery. I was hesitant but she urged me; regretfully, I turn to look back; a week later, Ah Gung died. Therefore, remember; you must "Never look back."

This was the end of an era. All of you children do not have to worry anymore; you cannot be deported. We were always afraid that we would be caught and deported to China. Now I am a seventy-something-year-old woman; I am not afraid anymore. I have children and grandchildren "born in America." The impossible dream has come true. They can't make me go back.

DEFINING MOMENTS: OF FAMILIES AND CULTURE

Like my mother, I too found my voice. While our contexts differed, much is strikingly the same. Like my mother, there are memories that are etched in my mind that I remember across time and space; these are defining moments that capture the essence of the moment and the experience of a lifetime. My voice expands hers so that there is new-found strength as we echo one another.

I remembered the day my mother received the letter of Ah Gung's death. It was almost a month after it happened; but it was her moment to mourn. She sent Ah Jeer to pick me up early from school so that we could grieve together. I was only 6 at the time; I felt little emotion not having known my grandfather. But we all felt the distress and pain as my mother cried over her loss and her inability to be by her father's side at the time of his death. All the pain in her life gushed forth as the final loss of her father forced her to reexperience her losses once again. The feelings of abandoning and being abandoned poured forth; she remembered the loss of her mother, her father's absence growing up, her leaving China and her family, and most of all, her leaving her son Sel Ming. We were too young to appreciate her pain; but we put pink yarn in our hair for the next week to show that we were in mourning.

We lived in Brooklyn, in a neighborhood where there were no other Asian faces. We felt an affinity with the one Filipino family there because we looked similar. There were so few Chinese in America that my mother would become so excited whenever she saw an Asian face on the street; she would rush up to them and start a conversation with them in Chinese. Her questions were standard: "Are you Chinese? What is your family name? What village in China are you from?" If they responded, she would proceed to engage them in a conversation as if she had found a long-lost friend. As children, we would cringe in embarrassment; my mother paid us no heed. The isolation my mother felt was so overwhelming, she threw all caution to the wind.

My memories are of the long and neverending hours of my parents working in the hot, sweaty laundry late into the night with the blinds drawn so as not to draw attention. They are of the Sunday family trips to Chinatown to connect with family members, who were really no more than distant relatives. Our extended family and cultural practices made everyone a relative, uncle, aunt, or cousin. Sunday was the only day of rest for my parents, and Chinatown was their only haven from the strange and seemingly unfriendly environment of Brooklyn. As we became teenagers, time seemed endless as we loitered on the streets of Chinatown on a Sunday afternoon. We belonged and stared at the tourists as objects of curiosity just as they did of us. These stories embellish those of my mother. They show the journey we took together and the transformation that occurred as we create new legends for our children and grandchildren.

Chinese Hand Laundry: Poverty

We owned a hand laundry, as most Chinese Americans did in those days. It was called the Louis Tong Hand Laundry. Many of the customers called my father Louie, thinking this was his name; he always greeted them in return and never corrected them. My parents worked together in the laundry during the early years of my childhood. Everything was done by hand in those days without the washers and dryers of today that led to the demise of hand laundries. My parents sorted the clothes, and then sent them to the wet wash. Shirts needed to be hand starched and ironed. There was a standard way to iron and fold the shirts before they were stacked and sorted for wrapping. The wrapped packages would be sorted by ticket number and stored on shelves for easy retrieval. As children, we helped with the wrapping, the cleanest and easiest part of the job. My parents reserved the smelly, more difficult part of the jobs for themselves. They were thankful for our help, but always afraid it would interfere with our studies. When business was good, my parents worked from 8 a.m. to 10 p.m. with little or no break. They dared not complain for fear of the lean times.

Sometimes there were customers set on creating trouble. They would make a false claim that we had ruined their shirts and insist on our paying for damages. With little command of English and a belief that the Chinese could never win a case in the legal system, my parents often felt demoralized by these experiences and sometimes physically threatened. The settlement was often unjust in my parents' eyes, but was made to avoid further litigation or threat. It was clear that the *lo faan* ["Mr. Foreigner" or whites] wanted to make sure we knew our place; the message was that no Chinese would get the better of them.

The cash register we had in the laundry was a simple wooden box under the ironing board. In order to open it, you had to pull three of the five levers underneath simultaneously. If you pulled the wrong ones, it would sound a musical note, but not open, alerting my parents to unauthorized entry. This was installed to prevent burglaries; my mother was hard of hearing and probably could not hear it ring, but it made her feel secure. Sometimes I would quietly open it while my mother was in the back room. I would pick out the coins that I thought would be less likely to be noticed and run out to buy candy. I made up a ritual so as not to feel guilty. Since we did not get an allowance as our white friends did, I felt justified in doing this.

Beebee Gow was the dog we had in the laundry, a lovable energetic mutt. My parents could never admit that they wanted a pet (it was too much of a luxury for poor Chinese immigrants) so they justified his presence as "raising a dog to watch over the house." Though we had many dogs, we never bought any of them. Beebee Gow (meaning Baby Dog) was inherited from my brother's godfather. When we took Beebee Gow in, we hated his name. We always tried to change it, but to no avail. We would call him Prince, King, or Beauty, names that we thought were more fitting for a dog. He would ignore our beckoning him to come, preferring to lie there looking at us. As soon as we called Beebee Gow, he immediately got up and came to us. We finally gave up, and he remained Beebee Gow for the rest of his life.

Beebee Gow was a free spirit; he did not like being chained in the laundry, although he was allowed to run loose in our enclosed yard several times a day. Whenever he was able to get loose from his chain, he would always try to run out into the streets. He would roam to unknown places for several hours, but would always come home. He got loose one day. In his enthusiasm to get out, he scaled the 3-foot-high counter in the laundry (as he often did) just as a customer was entering the laundry. The customer got the scare of his life as he saw this 50-pound dog lunging over the counter toward him. He frantically tried to dodge Beebee, only to realize that the dog had no interest in him. He only wanted to go out for a romp. Beebee Gow mirrored the feeling of my parents and many immigrants who feel trapped by their environment but always come home.

Our laundry was in Bedford-Stuyvesant, a ghetto in Brooklyn. Our neighborhood underwent rapid social change as each wave of new immigrants displaced the earlier ones; it went from Irish to Italian to

Puerto Rican. We lived on Ellery Street, a street ruled by the local gang of Ellery Bops. We would hear of rumbles and avoid getting involved. Sometimes gang members would befriend us and protect us from the taunting intimidation of others. Others would jeer at us, chanting racist remarks of: "Ching Chong" or "Chinita, Chinita" as we made our way to and from the subway five blocks away.

As the rate of burglaries rose, we installed iron gates over the open counter of the laundry and a mirror at the entrance to the laundry to enable my parents to look down the street from the inside. The mirror also served the purpose of giving my parents a view to the outside world as they slaved away in the laundry. We would come home from school and do our homework in the apartment above the laundry; my parents were always reminding us about how lucky we were not to have to live in the back of the laundry as so many Chinese immigrant families do. My parents were always working in the laundry downstairs. Sometimes, my sister and I would sneak out to the candy store. The mirror was a dead giveaway, so we figured out how to leave the house outside the view of this mirror by clinging to the building wall to avoid detection. Why did we do this? I don't know. My parents were always so busy working, they never noticed; but I was always delighted that I had pulled something over them.

Social Change: Impossible Dreams

As the neighborhood changed, so did the hand laundry business. It could no longer financially sustain the family. As children, we were not privy to these matters and did not understand the changes occurring around us. My father tried to start up other businesses in the hope of improving our lot. He was always very mechanical and handy, and enjoyed home fix-it projects. He first tried his hand at construction; however, his perfectionistic tendency made it impossible for him to make a living. He would take too long to complete a project. He then decided to start up another laundry out in Rockville Center on Long Island. It was his dream to move us out to a better neighborhood if he could make a go of it, but that was never to happen. He physically built the laundry from scratch himself and set up shop. He stayed there during the week and only came home on Sundays; he lived in the back of the laundry because he could not afford to rent an apartment. My mother remained alone, working the laundry in Brooklyn.

When this laundry venture failed, my father began working in restaurants to bring in extra income. The number of Chinese restaurants grew as Americans began to enjoy chow mein and chop suey dishes; most did not realize that no true Chinese would touch these Western dishes. We considered restaurant work a cut above the work of dealing with dirty laundry and envied our friends whose parents were restaurant owners. Since my father had no restaurant experience, he began as a dishwasher or third chef. As he was not one used to taking orders from others, the stress on him was profound. The handling of food and detergents were harsh on his hands; he developed dermatitis that affected his hands and legs. For many years thereafter, he was unable to work because of the sores oozing from his hands and legs. It seemed to be incurable, even after many visits to doctors; my father would bemoan the pain and debilitation he suffered. None of us recognized the psychosomatic aspects of his disorder and the manifestation of his suffering on his body. As a Chinese father and husband, he was too proud; he could not shirk from family responsibilities and could not tolerate the humiliation of not being in control of his fate.

Because my father was no longer there "to protect us" and because of the growing crime rate, we installed an intercom connecting the upstairs and laundry. The boldness (*dai om*) of my siblings and mother in foiling several burglary attempts was legendary in our family. One night, a burglar confronted my mother. With characteristic boldness, she ran to the intercom screaming for help. My brother, not heeding any danger, ran down to protect her. The burglar ran off, intimidated by their defiance. Another time, my sister confronted a would-be burglar in the laundry at the cash register. He ran off, with my 13-year-old sister in hot pursuit. She did justice to her well-earned reputation for spunkiness.

The harshness of living led to dreams of moving from the city. For my parents, the country was symbolic of the China they had left behind. They dreamed of the trees and the flowers, the freedom of open space. This was Islip out on Long Island. Convinced by our neighbors, my parents took a risk and bought a 2 ¼-acre lot in Islip to fulfill their dream. For some years, we would drive 3 hours each way out there every Sunday. It would be an all-day outing. My father would bring his hatchet to trim the trees. We would pack our food since we could not afford to go to restaurants. There were no facilities of any kind. We would hang out on this piece of land in the woods, and dream of the house that was never to be built. My father would draw detailed plans for its construction. He would clear the woods with his hatchet to see if the setting for the house would be just right. This was his dream to own a piece of the Good Earth, to live comfortably in retirement, and to be free. My father died in 1974, never living long enough to see the fulfillment of these dreams.

Drum, Bugle, and Fife Corp: A Chinese American Identity

Attending a Chinese language school was one of those defining moments that transformed us. As soon as my brother and sister were old enough, they were enrolled in a Chinese language school, which they attended after their regular studies in "American school." My parents wanted us to learn Chinese and to get a Chinese education even though they were too busy working in the laundry. Though my sister was merely 8 and my brother was 9, my parents had them travel alone to Chinatown in Manhattan by subway 5 days a week—a 45-minute ride each way with two transfers. Again, it was my brother's role at age 9 as the older brother to protect my sister. Being the youngest, I was not allowed to attend until 4 years later; at the age of 11, I was still considered too young. I begged to go to Chinese school.

Before starting Chinese school, I would listen with envy each night to the stories my brother and sister told about the friends they made and the fun they had. I was fascinated hearing about the ping-pong tournaments, volleyball games, school picnics, and drum and fife corps. I envied the fun my sister had simply throwing spitballs made of toilet paper on the bathroom walls. Most of all, Chinese school was a place where we shared a common experience of being Chinese—we had found our community and were no longer the exotic Chinese.

Most of our peers had a mediocre interest in the scholarship part of Chinese school, which used classical methods of teaching emphasizing rote memory and learning Chinese classics; some repeated first grade for several years before dropping out. The social relationships and the bonding with other Chinese American peers was transforming, and reinforced our cultural identities.

We all joined the drum, bugle, and fife corp whether or not we had any musical talent or interest. We did as we were told, marching in parades, celebrating the holidays; there was the Lantern Festival, Chinese New Year, and Double Ten Festival. We marched in the American parades and successfully competed in contests because our Chinese marching band was unique. Yet the corps instructor could never get the band past playing our four basic songs: "The Bells of St. Mary," "Auld Lang Syne,"

"Yankee Doodle," and "Battle Hymn of the Republic." Most of us were not serious musicians, having joined the band only for the social bonding. I became fife sergeant as the remaining senior member—ironic, because I only knew how to play these four songs.

As we participated in the annual Double Ten Festival, which celebrates the birth of the Republic of China, we never realized that this demonstrated the Chinese American community's support of the Nationalist Chinese government over communist China. We never really understood the fear of deportation experienced by my parents and others in the community if they were deemed a communist or were found to have falsified papers. We dutifully sang the "Star Spangled Banner" at assemblies in our American school, and "Sam Ming Ju Yee," the national anthem of the Republic of China at assemblies in our Chinese school; we never questioned the schism between the American and Chinese cultures, and the true lack of freedom felt by our parents.

All we knew was that we were supposed to "be Chinese; speak Chinese," a strong recurring message from our families and Chinese elders, for fear that we would lose our Chinese heritage. During the melting pot era of the 1950s in America, American patriotism was the strong recurring message of our American schools and society. Yet, there were daily reminders that Chinese Americans were not truly Americans, which was embodied in the recurrent question, "Are you Chinese or Japanese?" by white strangers. At the same time, our Chinese elders would call us American-born Chinese *jook sing*, a rather derogatory name referring to the hollow part of the bamboo tree, meaning our brain. Instead, we wore this label with pride in arrogant defiance of their derogation; we knew who we were.

Being Chinese American was an experience of schisms and contradictions. We spoke Toisanese at home (a village dialect spoken by uneducated people), read Cantonese at Chinese school (a city dialect of the more refined), and sang the Chinese national anthem in Mandarin (the national dialect of the scholars). We spoke Chinese at home at the insistence of our parents and English at American school at the insistence of our teachers. We were told to be integrated in our identity as one person. While our American schools emphasized patriotism, every year during Chinese New Year we were asked to tell the other kids in class about being Chinese. I remember being puzzled once when a friend's father drove me home; I was sitting in the back of the car, and he said, "I can't tell that you are Chinese by hearing you speak." Was this patronizing or complimentary? Did he expect me to speak broken English, although I was born in America?

CHINATOWN: FAMILY AND COMMUNITY BONDS

We roamed the streets of Chinatown as teenagers—five short blocks along Mott Street. It was a community; it was ours. We named each of different groups who "hung out" together. There was "the 37 crowd" who lived at 37 Mott Street; the Transfiguration crowd, who attended the church; the Vikings, an athletic volleyball team, and Poy Ching, the social club. As our parents made their Sunday outings to the clan associations, we made it out to church in Chinatown to meet with friends and hang out. It would take us several hours to walk down the five short blocks of Mott Street as we stopped along the way to chat with friends and make new acquaintances. The *lo faan* tourists came to stare at the exotic sights of Chinese people and roasted meats in the store windows, awed by the neon lights of Chinatown at night. We would greet the Chinese elders on the streets who walked with a slow shuffle with eyes downcast; there were the sojourners who lived alone in New York's Chinatown.

The Family Clan Association: Bachelor Husbands

As children, we took the subway every Sunday to go out to New York's Chinatown to hang out at Cher-Long-Fong (the Lau clan association). This was the life behind the neon signs; this was community, family, and culture. The association members were bachelor husbands, sojourners—men who worked as laundry owners with wives still in China, ever hopeful that they would be reunited one day. China became communist after 1949, so little communication with their wives were possible; most of the men were more concerned with their families than with the politics. They would spend their Sundays talking, sharing stories of China and bemoaning their plight in America.

The conversations at the clan association often drifted to reminiscing about the good old days in China and the people's dreams of returning to an idyllic China. The lychees and fruits they remembered were always sweeter and fresher, the flowers always more beautiful, and the scenery far surpassed any of that in America; the illusion of the peach orchard in the Jade Mountain of their minds was friendlier than anywhere in America. But the harshness of poverty in China was also remembered for its consequences of starvation and illness; conversations frequently ended with sighs of relief and appreciation that at least there was food to eat here.

We were educated from listening to these conversations about *tiel meng,* one's life and fate, and how some people were *ji-woon* (unlucky) while others were *herng-fook* (prosperous). Not much was to be done about fate. The elders endlessly bemoaned their fate in America struggling to make a living. Amidst this anguish were their dreams of returning to China in retirement to live in comfort and with respect in their home villages. This was the perpetual dream of my father as he and others hoped to make the hardship and struggle of working in a laundry more bearable. The elders would commiserate together, believing there was no escape from their fate of struggle and from the poverty bondage that they felt.

The clan association was also the place where we children learned about health problems—gallstones the size of rocks, sugar in the urine—or heard about concubines (Uncle So-and-So was a judge in China so he could afford to have so many wives, the second wife here is angry now because Uncle So-and-So is bringing over his first wife). We pretended to play or to sit obediently as we listened with awe to these stories.

As children, we often did not understand the Chinese elders. Their habits and disdain for the *bak guey* (white devils), and their mistrust, poker face demeanor, or obsequiousness when dealing with whites contrasted so starkly with their bold and energized demeanor when talking among themselves in the privacy of the *gung si fong* (clan association). The stories of these Chinese elders were colorful, but spoke of a wall, or perhaps a brocade curtain, that separated them from mainstream America; it was a curtain through which they could not escape or leave. They were bound by the oppression of racism, their psychological isolation, and the burden of poverty as they etched their lives out in America. Most recounted the infamous signs at foreigner hotels in Shanghai, China following World War II, "Chinese and dogs not allowed." This story was used to exemplify the racist American attitudes toward Chinese people.

Whenever my father was asked what his line of work was, his response was always the same: "What is there to do? I work a laundry!" Many of the Chinese immigrant men would say with frustration, "the *lo faan* will not let you do anything else." When feeling more cynical and pessimistic, they would chide you with a discouraging tone: "Look in the mirror at your face!" This meant you could never change or hide the fact that you are Chinese.

Early Toisanese immigrants remember the feudal governments in China, while later Hong Kong immigrants remember British colonialism and government corruption—all sought a safe haven from oppression. In the privacy of the *gung si fong* (clan association) we heard stories from the Chinese elders about brainwashing and execution in the new communist regime; they weighed this political oppression against racism in America. They debated what was needed to bring China out of a feudal era.

The men always talked of sending money back to their families, and their continuing obligation to the families they left behind. Yet all lived in impoverished conditions themselves—either in the backs of their laundries or sharing rooms with other bachelor husbands.

Whenever a letter from China would arrive, it would be circulated at the clan association. It would be read and discussed by those in the room, for this was an opportunity to connect with those in China even if it was not one's own family. Those who were more literate would read for those who were less literate. There was shared anger when relatives were overly demanding, usually asking for money because they believed life was so good in America. Everyone had the opportunity to give an opinion and advice. There was news about family births, marriages, and deaths.

My parents' letters came from Sel Ming (my brother) and Dai Q (my maternal uncle); it was through these letters that my parents would attempt to parent and discipline Sel Ming from across the ocean. The letters from Dai Q would report his misbehavior and his unwillingness to study while the letters from Sel Ming would plead for a speedy reunion. My parents would write back to scold him and insist on his listening to Dai Q and Dai Kim.

It was a vibrant atmosphere with multiple conversations in this small space. The decibel levels rose as men dropped in and out of this gathering place on a Sunday afternoon—their only day of rest. I never noticed that my mother was the only woman in the room, and that those who talked to us had crossed the boundaries of the gender divide. I learned a lot on these afternoons as I sat obediently near my parents. Conversation was not censored and there were no toys nearby; instead, we listened to this adult conversation and learned vicariously the lessons of life—through the fears, dreams, and suffering of these early Chinese American immigrants.

No *guey lo* (demon) ever came to visit the *gong si fong;* none was ever invited. Our clan association consisted of three small rooms in a railroad-style apartment; behind the small 15-by-10-foot living room where everyone congregated was a small kitchen and sleeping quarters for bachelor men needing inexpensive, transient living quarters. The association assisted in finding people jobs, making loans, providing social networking, and giving mutual support. They sometimes settled disputes since Chinese immigrants would not trust the justice system of the American courts.

The Emergence of Women

My mother was one of the first wives in the clan association; we were the only children. Some elders talked with us, others talked around us, believing that women and children had their proper place and were not to be heard. There was Mong Hong Bak (Uncle Mong Hong), a nice, gentle uncle who would talk to us; he was always smiling and might give us a nickel for candy; we would always anticipate this eagerly. There was a younger uncle whom we called Gee Bak Gai, nicknamed Pigsy since he was fat with a huge stomach. He always seemed to be asleep as he sat and listened to the conversation. There were the gambling elders, who played 13-card poker, the favorite card game of Toisanese men; they played energetically in the corner of this 15-by-10-foot room while carrying on exclusive conversations. They smoked heavily and swore intensely as they won or lost a hand, for these were the signs of masculinity. For the most part, they ignored us as we did them, since children and women did not fit into their circle of interaction. Every once in a while, one would win a big hand and give us children a dollar or two to extend his luck.

This was home base for my parents on a Sunday afternoon in Chinatown for many years. They would do their weekly shopping for Chinese goods unavailable in the markets in Brooklyn, and return to the clan association with their food for a final chat before heading home. They would visit other clan associations, all of which possessed the same ambience.

There was one Foo Nul Foong (Women's Association) that my mother would visit; I never understood why my father remained at Cher Long Foong and urged her to go by herself. I now realize that this was a new alternative for women to the *gung si fong,* or clan associations for men. It was one of the first women's associations (as the name suggests, although I did not understand its English meaning at the time) to emerge in Chinatown—begun by and for immigrant women back in the late 1950s as more women immigrated to join their husbands. My mother would enjoy her visits here in a room filled with women and children, unlike the gambling den of Cher Long Foong that my father frequented.

The Family Clan: Honorific Titles

The family clan or extended family is the underlying backbone of Chinese culture. Honorific titles designated every familial relationship. Once a relationship was formed, honorific titles of "uncle" were created to designate the relationship; thus, the titles Ah Suk and Ah Bahk

(Younger and Elder Paternal Uncle) were given to friends in relationship to the two men. Neighbors coming from the same village or clans in China were designated as Hong Ah Suk or Hong Ah Bahk.

While our extended family in America was often several generations removed, my father would honor the relationship by emphasizing that they were our closest relatives here in America. When meeting anyone new, we always discussed the order of the relationship between my father and the other man in order to decide the honorific title, which we were to use in addressing one another.

In the 1940s and 1950s, my mother was one of few Chinese women in America, since most of the wives had yet to immigrate. She considered herself fortunate to be here. She always took it upon herself to make extra pastries during the Chinese holidays to give to the bachelor husbands who did not have their wives here to make it for them. During Chinese New Year, we would deliver these pastries, and looked forward to the *hung bow* (red envelopes with money) that we would receive from friends and relatives in return. We were all taught to make an initial protest that it was unnecessary, so as not to appear greedy; we always knew our acceptance of the *hung bow* would be insisted upon; we would be complimented for our good manners. We were taught to always properly thank them using the proper honorific title that they had been given. We could see the delight in the elders as we came with these presents. They saw in us what we did not: the future and hope that they envied for themselves. We spoke English; we could negotiate the mainstream environment in ways they felt they never would. This was our extended family.

While Cher Long Foong was the clan association where my parents connected and gained support, there was another family clan. As discussed earlier, my father was born a Lau, was adopted as a Lee, and immigrated to America under papers as a Lau. Initially, there were no Lee relatives here in America. After some Lee relatives immigrated here in the 1960s, my father felt torn. He feared the Lau clan who had befriended him and helped him get started would disapprove and reject him for being disloyal if he now associated with the Lees. On the other hand, he feared the Lee clan would accuse him of being ungrateful in returning to the Lau clan. To resolve this dilemma, we maintained dual identities and social ties with both clans; however, we were coached never to mention that we were a Lau in front of our Lee relatives and vice versa. As children, we walked around with this secret, never really understanding why it was all so important; we knew to switch identities—our surnames—depending on whom we were with.

As an adult, I visited some maternal relatives in Canada with my maternal uncle, Poy Q. When asked my last name, I stammered, forgetting which one I was to use, and said Lau. My uncle gently corrected me, saying we were Lee, attributing my confusion to my ignorance as a *jook sing* (American-born Chinese).

We were always switching identities. In addition to our two clans, we also had paper relatives whom we sometimes visited; we treated them with more distance since there was no "real" family relationship. My parents always feared being deported. According to our immigration papers, we were Lau in English; but because of my father's loyalty to his adoptive family, we were Lee in Chinese. We were coached that we must never tell this to *lo faan* because it would jeopardize our immigration status. We carefully memorized our paper identities in case we were asked, and were cautioned about being probed too much about our identities by white people.

This all changed after the Family Reunification Act of 1965, which enabled Chinese families to reunite. For years, we were trained to hide our true identities; now we needed to come clean if we had any hope of bringing our families over from China. My father "confessed," as did so many other Chinese immigrants. He could finally tell who he was. My father then legally changed his name to Kim Lau Lee to honor his adopted parents and return to his rightful namesake while retaining his biological ties. This act threw all of us children into a new identity crisis—to integrate the various parts of our identities that had been kept separate all of our lives. This act made it possible for my mother to begin proceedings to bring over Sel Ming, the son she had left in China over 25 years before, though this would not happen for another 25 years.

Our Chinese American Culture: Training Character

My mother enjoyed good music and good stories. The classical Chinese stories discussed earlier were part of our moral training, as they were for most Chinese immigrant children. The "Three Moves of Mencius" was frequently told to us to celebrate a mother's wisdom, the value placed on scholarship, and the importance of the environment.

For a time, my mother took us to the Chinese movies on a weekly basis. Many of the martial arts movies featured feats that defy gravity and fighters with speeds and skills that bordered on fantasy. We would laugh in disbelief while my mother would explain the use of the wind and inner Qi (force) in Chinese culture as true power and strength brought about by vigorous training. It was not until the Bruce Lee and

Jackie Chan martial arts movies became popular in the West that we could appreciate this aspect of Chinese culture.

When live Cantonese Chinese opera came to town, we attended these performances, which were known as *dai hay* or Big Performances. My sister hated the opera because of its jarring, falsetto high tones, which she described as shrieks; it gave her headaches. Afterward, my mother would teach me some of the songs in Mandarin. She always took delight in being able to speak Mandarin, which she had learned while living in Nanjing; together we would listen to the music and rehearse the lyrics. There were several songs we sang together over and over again. She was delighted, and so proud when I could finally sing two of these songs on my own, although I could never remember what the words meant.

Cantonese Chinese opera, martial arts, and classic Chinese stories contrasted with our interest in Elvis Presley and the rock and roll music of the 1950s and 1960s. The age of rock and roll brought in the make-up, crinolines, and teased hair that was the craze during our adolescence. My sister and I would wear eight starched crinolines under full circle skirts. We wore these on a daily basis, carefully layering each crinoline upon one another to fluff them out, and stood out like Chinese southern belles. During our adolescence, there were dress-up dance parties that we attended; to these, we often wore the Chinese *cheong saam* (mandarin collar dress with side slits). These visual contrasts in music, story, and dress illustrated our seamless switches between Chinese and American cultures.

Chinese theaters were notorious for the noise made by theatergoers who carried on conversations and socialized while the performances were in progress. While my sister complained of the noise of Cantonese Chinese opera, my parents complained of the noise of rock and roll. My sister and I would go into the record store and spend hours selecting a hit tune to buy on a 45 rpm record. We resonated with the liveliness, loudness, and rhythm of rock and roll music and tried to remain oblivious to the gripping fears of the McCarthy era and a racist society.

In addition to the "classic" Chinese stories that were used for moral training, my mother told stories of her children to illustrate character—an important focus in Chinese culture. These stories defined a moment and captured our character at critical moments in our lives. As she retold these stories to friends and relatives, it ingrained in us an image of what she saw and expected of us.

My brother was the "protective one," as any good brother should be. When he was no more than 3 or 4 years old, I had put a hook in my eye. Seeing the danger, he ran over and pulled it out of my eye, leaving a scar that I still have. To my parents, my brother had taken action to save me. The demands of Chinese culture on the son and firstborn are high. He is the one to carry the family line and fulfill the obligation and debt of the family. My brother's adolescence was turbulent, because the tension between him and my father escalated over the demands and expectations between a Chinese father and his son.

My sister, on the other hand, was the "spunky" one. She was the one who would stand up to my father when no one else would. He was a tyrant in the manner of a Chinese father who expected unquestioning obedience and respect. When she was no older than 10, my father lost his temper with her and threatened to hit her. This was no casual threat, since my parents kept a switch over the door as a visual symbol of their authority. This switch was used periodically for physical discipline, but the threat was more frightening than the reality. My sister retaliated with her own threat "to pluck his eyes out and dip them in white sugar for eating." My father was reportedly so impressed with her audacity that he let his guard down and laughed.

I was remembered for my generosity (being *dai len*). One day at Cher Long Foong, my brother, sister, and I had all come in with ice cream cones. My sister dropped her cone and tried to take away my brother's cone. As he started to cry, I was said to have gone over to my sister and offer her my ice cream cone. All the relatives watching were impressed with how I could be so *dai len* at the age of 5. I, however, remember my curiosity. When I was about 5, I was once home alone. I climbed up on the kitchen table and stuck my finger into an open, live electric socket to see what it would do. I got the shock of my life and was so scared that I never dared to tell anyone.

Through the music and stories, we became Chinese Americans. They challenged our innocence and fueled our hopes. The curtain that closed China to Chinese American immigrants due to communism in 1949 fueled a paranoia among white Americans and fear among Chinese Americans who were struggling to survive in a racist America. The Family Reunification Act of 1965 brought in new hope and a new idealism, only to be shattered with the assassinations of President John F. Kennedy and civil rights leader Martin Luther King. It was not until President Richard Nixon's trip to China in 1971 that our worlds were brought together once again. During our childhood, we thought communism was bad and democracy was good. We did not talk about certain things. We pretended they did not exist. With Nixon's trip to China, suddenly it was okay to talk about communism, to visit China, and to have hopes of reuniting with family.

My parents visited China the very next year, living out their long-awaited dream of returning to China. Like so many of their fellow immigrants, they visited in search of the China they had left behind, and to reunite with family. The pictures of my parents in Mao Tse Tung jackets were an anomaly we could not reconcile. What my parents found was a China vastly different from what they had left behind. They realized that the China they sought was with them all along—in their hearts and in the Chinatown community that they had created in America.

CHAPTER 6

Traveling to the Future: Connecting with the Past

HISTORY AND NOW: ANCESTRY REVISITED

Though her immigration from Toisan spanned 8,000 miles across the ocean, my mother dared not venture beyond the confines of her Chinatown community without someone to accompany her during her 55 years in America. Since she lived in Brooklyn, her primary journey was to go to Chinatown in New York City. Our vacations brought her to places as far away as her hometown of Nanjing, China; as magnificent as the Great Wall of China; as foreign as the streets of Paris; and as awesome as the volcano eruptions on the big island of Hawaii. We traveled north to Ottawa, Canada where her half-sister had immigrated; south to Florida; west to California where the Lau clan now resided; and east to China. As we visited the four corners of the earth, my mother would exclaim, "In my days as a laundrywoman, these are places I never even saw in my dreams."

Vacations: Intergenerational Bonding

And so my mother and I journeyed together. Vacations became an avenue for us to remain connected. As my mother joined my husband and two children for our annual vacations, the generations bonded. I got to see my mother while she became the mother to my husband and the grandmother to my children that we in our childhood never had as an opportunity.

Her stories, as recounted in the oral history of this book, filled our time as her voice connected with the voices from past; and we bonded through the images in our present. I heard the wisdom of her simple words; I heard the anguish of her experience; I heard the bondage of her life. As we traveled, I saw the world through both her eyes and mine. I saw in her the pioneering spirit but the villager at heart. I felt her plight of lifelong longing and guilt for those she left behind; I felt her neverending hope for us, her children, not to have to suffer as she did. The paradoxes between us were many. I had a doctorate, while my mother had only a sixth-grade education. We were both well traveled, yet she was confined to Chinatown while my horizons had expanded. We grew up in two different worlds; she after the turn of the 20th century in the first year of the Republic of China, me a post–World War II baby. Yet it was she who mentored me.

The civil rights movement and the women's movement of the 1960s raised our hopes, while the assassinations of Martin Luther King and John F. Kennedy shattered them. The 1960s and 1970s were transformational—the era of the Vietnam War, the flower children, the peace movement, and the Me Generation.

My mother died in 1994, hit by a car as she crossed the street to go home to Confucius Plaza in the supposedly protected confines of Chinatown. Following her death, these renewed ties were ended, as I would no longer travel that journey with her again. I struggled with how to make sense of the senseless, just as we as a nation years later struggled with senseless assassinations and terrorism. So traumatized were we by my mother's death that we could barely cross the street again without fear and pain, knowing that her life ended in such tragedy.

Seventy-Two Adventures: Completing the Journey

We visited China together with my mother, husband, and 3-year-old son while I was pregnant in 1981. My mother had waited for this trip since my father's death in 1974. Her trip to China with my father in 1972 had been curtailed because of his health.

His trip back to China at the age of 72 after almost 40 years was a disappointment he never openly admitted. He found he no longer belonged. The dream that had kept him going, that had enabled him to struggle with the poverty, the racism, and the hardships of making a living in America was empty. Suddenly he could see through the embellishments and myths he had created about how idyllic life would be in China when he returned.

My mother looked to me to complete the journey that was never finished with my father. For my mother, this was a dream come true. Even though she was from China, she had never "seen" China. As a child, she was told of the wonders of China, but she never dreamed that she would see the magnificence of the Great Wall, the natural beauty of Guilin, the industrialized Shanghai, the celebrated beauty of the women in Hangzhou, or the opulence of the Summer Palace. We were both in awe as we approached the Summer Palace; here were a 74-year-old grand-mother and pregnant mother in sweltering 90-degree heat together try-ing to climb the 1,000 steps of their journey leading to the top.

I was amazed at Shanghai's industrialization and the Western influ-ence in the architecture, while my mother remembered how the Western powers had been so cunning in reaching an agreement with China to divide up Shanghai after World War II. According to my mother, the Western powers told China that they just wanted to occu-py land the size of a water buffalo. China acquiesced, only to find that the Western powers had cut up the sinews of the water buffalo into one long string, and stretched it into one large circle, thereby occupying all of Shanghai. To add insult to injury, they then prohibited the Chinese from using the public gardens, with posted signs that said "No dogs or Chinese allowed." As her self-esteem and national pride swelled up, I could feel the shame and injury in my mother's tone of voice.

The trip to China was an opportunity for reunions as much as it was for seeing the sights. In Nanjing, my mother reunited with Sel Ming, her son whom she had seen only once after she left him in 1939, 42 years before. I met my older brother for the first time when he was 47. He was married with 4 grown children. Although we were brother and sister, our lives could not have been more different. Our communica-tion difficulties could not be more symbolic, as his children and I spoke different dialects. They knew little about my life in the United States and could not fathom the amenities to which we were accustomed. Though Sel Ming now lived a middle-class life, his family had no run-ning water in the house; toilet facilities were a block away in an out-house; and their one sink for a family of 6 was outside the front door. One loft served as the sleeping quarters for the entire family, while the floors were natural dirt floors. Suddenly I understood the books I used to read at Chinese school; the books described spraying down a floor to clean it and keep the dust down.

After spending a week with Sel Ming, the pain my mother felt in having to leave him once again is rekindled in my memory. I could feel her anguish, and imagine the resurgence of that moment when he woke up to find her gone. This moment resurrected all the abandonment guilt she felt, and her helpless inability to change her fate.

Almost 25 people came to the airport, waiting all day to meet us (because I had not wanted to inconvenience them by telling them my flight arrival time). This was a different sense of time. Parading before me now were all the relatives in the stories from my mother's past including Ah Yee, my mother's half-sister, and her husband Yee Cherng (Husband of Younger Maternal Aunt), and the children of Dai Q, my mother's brother. All of Dai Q's children had become doctors or pharmacists and were well educated; my Yee Cherng was an accountant. I saw my mother stuck in a time warp; she was the one who had the courage to venture overseas.

We had all heard stories of one another through the letters my mother had written over the years. Now the stories we exchanged about our lives gave a new sense of reality; my mother's life in the laundry was not one of luxury or comfort. Although she had been the one to provide them with financial support, their educational achievements matched mine.

As we toured Nanjing, my mother sought out the building that had once been owned by my grandfather, Ah Gung. My mother had heard that property in China could be reclaimed by overseas Chinese; as we searched, my relatives quietly told me that under communism, the government had taken over all properties. My mother remembered anew the atrocities of the Japanese during the rape of Nanking. It was clear that she was still traumatized by her escape after more than 40 years.

My mother also learned how much she had changed. Although we viewed my mother as so Chinese, my Yee Cherng said it was clear she was from the United States. When I asked him how people could tell, he said with affection, "Look at the way she dresses. It is risqué showing her shoulders at her age. And all that color." My mother was wearing a sleeveless, conservative (or so I thought) gray-and-black print dress. I then realized that women over 50 in China wore nothing but plain black or brown and covered their shoulders even in very hot weather.

One Hundred Years of Good Fortune

One hundred is the number Chinese use when they want to give you a blessing. It is comparable to infinity. So it is common to wish "May you live 100 years!" When we left Nanjing, Ah Yee gave my mother a beautiful, satin brocade cloth embroidered with 100 children. It was her wish for my mother to be blessed with a 100 offspring (usually including grandchildren and great-grandchildren).

In Beijing, we met with the eldest son of my Dai Q, Ah Fei Gong. For my mother, it was to be her last reunion; she treated the visit as a reconnection with family whom she had never expected to see again. Her special bond to Fei Gong as the oldest son of her elder brother and primary link in the ancestral line to her father was evident. In return, Fei Gong treated her and us with the utmost of respect; she was his Dai Goo (Eldest of the Younger Paternal Aunt) of his father who had already passed away. He escorted us to the Great Wall of China and the Heavenly Temple of Beijing. Fei Gong's behavior was consistent with Confucian principles of ancient China, where the emperor was regarded as the "Son of Heaven," who administered matters on earth on behalf of the heavenly authority.

Volcanic Eruptions

We visited the big island in Hawaii while the volcano of Hilo was active and erupted lava was flowing from the mountaintop to the sea. Since I did not have the Chinese vocabulary to inform my mother where we were going, I could not tell her what we were about to see. The sight of the erupting volcano was beyond her wildest imagination. At first, she wondered what the fiery, soft, molten gray lava was. When I pointed from where it was flowing, there was disbelief at first. She said, "These are wonders about which you hear; never ones that I thought I would see." My own awe in seeing this once-in-a-lifetime event was enhanced—sandwiched between the awe of my mother and that of my children. My mother reacted like a child—the grandmother more enthralled than my children at this natural wonder. She rushed to examine the lava, and to collect what she could as a memoir to bring home.

Although she was confined to Chinatown, my mother had collected the names and addresses of relatives or friends from her past who had immigrated to different cities in the United States. As we reached our destination, she often asked me to look them up. As we traveled, she had the opportunity to revisit and reconnect with people from her past while I had the opportunity to put names and faces to the stories I had heard from my mother when I was growing up. Over the years, we reunited with Wong friends and relatives in Vancouver, Toronto, Seattle, Los Angeles, San Francisco, Ottawa, and Texas. These were relatives, her childhood friends, and her village sisters (*hong ah jeer*) from Hoiping village. One *hong ah jeer*, in her 80s, was shocked and delighted to see my mother; she reminisced with my mother and shared stories of the village, of their youth, and how they had been so close that they shared a bed together. As I heard their affirmation of my mother's experiences and watched the glow in my mother's face, I connected with the past and revisited my ancestry. Our history was now in the present. As I watched my mother's face beam with joy and listened to her voice fill with excitement, I said to myself, "These are experiences I would only have dreamed of."

On our visit to Los Angeles in 1992, I was in for the surprise of my life. We had looked up a relative with Ah Koon Seem, my aunt from the Lau clan. The visit was quite enjoyable, as my mother once again exchanged stories of life in China. Because of my mother's poor hearing, Ah Koon Seem told me (rather than my mother) that she wanted to bring us to visit some relatives. Not able to keep the names and honorific titles of extended family relatives from the Lau and Lee clans straight, and hampered by my need to translate Chinese names into their English equivalent, I acquiesced. I did not fully realize the significance of the people we were to meet until we sat around the table in the restaurant. Suddenly I realized that we were talking to my father's nephew, Sam Suk's son, and my father's half sister, Ah Dai Goo from the Lau clan, the biological family who had abandoned him as an infant. In my youth, these relatives would write to my father with hardship stories asking for money. Always angered by these letters because my father believed the stories were embellished, my father nevertheless always sent them some money. Neither my siblings nor I ever knew that they had made it to the United States and were living in Los Angeles. Sam Suk was infamous for his cunning and his exploitation of others for money. Because of my father's loyalty to his birth parents, he gave in to these appeals for money.

For the first time I watched my mother freeze in her social interaction. Typically energetic and overjoyed at meeting with people from her past and always ready to share stories and memories, I saw my mother become silent and angry. I was bewildered and did not understand. After we left, my mother expressed her anger. She reminded me of how her Lau Lo Yeer (Lau father-in-law) had accused her of being restless and not watchful of the home as she waited for my father in China; this implied that she was not virtuous. My mother emphatically said she had no interest in meeting them. Only then did I realize how much this had been an assault to her character and integrity. As generous and forgiving as my mother was, this was unforgivable.

We traveled to Ottawa, Canada in 1993 and reunited for the last time with my mother's half sister, Ah Yee. My mother and Ah Yee were able to transcend the past, reconnect in the present, and bond as sisters. On this visit, we had reunited four generations of children, grandchildren, and great-grandchildren with my mother and Ah Yee. After my mother's death, these trips ended.

Reunion After 50 Years

Through the years, my mother always remembered Sel Ming—her son, my brother. It was she who reminded us to send him money for Chinese New Year. It was she who wrote to him to keep in touch. She never gave up her motherly guidance and never forgot her obligation and promise. After my father's death, she renewed her vigor in fulfilling that promise, with my brother's help. Since Sel Ming had been adopted as an infant, my mother had to legally prove that he was my father's son. Her reliance on dates was committed to memory rather than paper, and was sometimes contradictory. Through her perseverance, she finally reunited with him 50 years later when he came to live in the United States at age 55.

By then, he was a grandfather. Sel Ming arrived with his wife to rejoin my mother. Both could now complete their journey; my mother had completed her obligation. She had absolved her guilt. Having provided financial support to him all his life, she now felt it was his turn to show the filial piety due to her as his mother. It was her expectation that he become all that she expected of her eldest son.

For Sel Ming, the 50 years of separation, of yearning to be with his mother, of coming to America to join his family were now over. We can only guess what his dreams might have been about his missed opportunities that we, his siblings, enjoyed in the United States. But the pain and anguish of mother–son separation over the course of 50 years do not disappear with a reunion. As reality set in, it became clear that the reunion could not heal these wounds. Sel Ming and his wife lived with my mother to get themselves settled, but the mother–son relationship that had been absent during the 50 years of separation was simulated.

As they renegotiated their mother–son relationship, now as great-grandmother and grandfather, the anguish remained. My mother expected him to be grateful for the years she had spent in anguish to keep her promise to him. She had supported him for years long after she stopped supporting her children in the United States. She had suffered much hardship fighting with my father to keep her promise. Sel Ming, on the other hand, expected her to make up for the years he had lost, for the years he had waited, for his years without a mother. He observed the huge material contrasts between himself and us and could not help but think what his life would have been like if she had not left him. Now that mother and son were reunited, they could finally be angry at each other. My mother could never understand Sel Ming's anguish; she believed it is a son's obligation to honor his parents. My father never lived to see this reunion.

NEVERENDING THEMES: IMMIGRANT BONDS

The themes of separation, loss, guilt, and obligation are never-ending. As immigrants make their journey, immigrant families bond across generations. Yet it is also these very bonds that put us in bondage, linking us inexplicably to an inescapable fate, making obligation and guilt lifelong things. As Chinese immigrants leave their families, their culture, and their country behind, the abandonment guilt is often long-lasting. I watched as my mother struggled with this guilt, a common bond among immigrants that leads to continual anguish.

Obligation: A Lifelong Debt

Family obligation is a lifelong debt and results in lifelong bonds. My mother was unrelenting in her loyalty and bond to my maternal uncles, Poy Q, Gong Q, and Hing Q, who escaped Nanjing together with her; they were actually my mother's first cousins. I did not fathom the significance of these relationships when we first met in Hong Kong. She fulfilled her obligation by helping to sponsor them to the United States. In return, they understood their obligation to honor her in the United States until her death. This mutual expectation of honor and obligation in Chinese families is lifelong. My uncles would always bring her a chicken for her birthday and periodically treat her to dim sum; their wives also continued to honor her and repay the debt.

Sons and Mothers: Fulfilling a Promise

My mother's guilt over leaving her son behind was pervasive in our lives. Her stories were replete with references to him. She tried to be a parent to him through letters from across the ocean. She wanted to ensure that relatives in Toisan and Nanjing would protect him, and sent them money gifts as payment for their work and her debt. This lifelong bond and bondage that she felt was the basis for arguments that she and my father had over its drain on our meager resources. My father was often angry over the demands made by relatives who were caring for Sel Ming to materially benefit from my mother's guilt and affection. Nothing could sway her from fulfilling her promise to bring him to the United States.

A Son's Obligation: A Parent's Expectation

Sons are favored in Chinese families; mine was no different. My brother in America held the esteemed role and burden of being the eldest son to carry on the family name. While he got the benefits of not doing household chores, he also bore the burden of having to protect and represent the family—this was *yen goy* (expected) according to my parents. While he was the one to receive the lion's share of any resources compared to us daughters, he was expected to demonstrate his fiial piety and obedience to my parents.

True to Chinese custom, he and my mother shared a special bond. My sister and I resented this preferential treatment, believing my brother was getting away with things. Only in adulthood did we realize how my brother envied the bonding my sister and I shared as women and how he missed not having a brother.

Adoption: Separation Anxiety

As human beings make transitions, there is often separation anxiety associated with leaving behind and embracing new environments. Families and communities are the very essence of identity, especially within Chinese families, which connect family lines across villages, generations, and oceans. This is what results in the creation of Chinatowns, the inability to separate from them, and the perpetuation of cultural practices in the host country long after they are given up in the country of origin. The need for constancy results in the narrowing of one's boundaries.

Given the high rate of infant mortality and poverty in China, adoptions to replace a child who died were common. They were also intended to reduce the economic burden to a family. Yet the premium placed on a woman's fertility, and the importance of producing sons to continue the family line meant that there was also shame associated with adoptions—shame of abandonment, infertility, and rejection.

In our Lau/Lee family, there is at least a four-generation legacy of adoption. My father was adopted like his father; my brother, Sel Ming, was adopted, as was my son Scott. My father maintained a dual relationship with both clans, but proclaimed his lifelong loyalty to his adoptive parents. Feelings of separation anxiety associated with adoption compound experiences of loss associated with immigration.

One of the legendary stories my father told was of his adoption and loyalty to his Lee adoptive parents. He maintained dual relationships with both clans, keeping them separate and "secret" from one another for fear that his loyalty would be questioned. His obligation and loyalty to his adoptive parents and the Lee clan was permanent until his death.

While adoption was often a stigma in both the East and the West, knowledge of the birth parents was not uncommon, given that villages were organized around family clans. Given the emphasis on family lineage, loyalty, and obligation, adoptions were often kept secret from the adopted child for fear of losing their loyalty. We had a cousin who was never told of his adoption. Raised by his mother, he was left behind when she reunited with his father. When his mother tried to sponsor him to the United States as her son, she had to explain to the immigration authorities how she could have borne a son when her husband was already in the United States when he had been conceived. Rather than admitting to adopting him, she chose to bear the "lesser shame" of admitting that she had had an affair. This was her bondage as she struggled with her fear that her son would leave her if he discovered the truth.

I told my son of his adoption early on. Yet when my younger son Stephen was born, Scott, at the age of 3, asked about "when he was in my tummy." Not wanting to traumatize him following the recent birth of a sibling, I chose to be silent at great discomfort, since his adoption had never been a secret. One day at the age of 5 while I was bathing the two, he once again asked, "Tell me about when I was in your tummy." This time, I told him, "You never were." In apparent shock, he said, "Do you mean you are not my mommy?" I said, "No, I am your mommy. I just did not give birth to you." Scott was very pensive that night. When I went to wake him in the morning, he related to me, "Mommy, I saw this last night. There were two mommies and they came together and became one." He gestured with his hands and showed me how he had integrated the issue of his adoption. Once considered a stigma, adoption has taken on different meaning in all cultures. When my relatives heard that I had told my son of his adoption, I was warned that this might affect his feelings of love and loyalty toward me.

The process of immigration often involves psychological processes not unlike that of adoption. All immigrants adopt a culture. They adopt the dress, behaviors, and beliefs of the host culture while retaining aspects of their culture of origin. For some, it is just the exterior. For others, it is obliteration of the interior. For still others, it is the bringing together as one, like the yin and the yang.

THE SEARCH AND THE JOURNEY

Journey to the West: Immigration

And like the Monkey King in his journey to the west, all Chinese immigrants made their journey to the West and submitted to trials in

Western society to reach enlightenment. Early Toisanese immigrants were known for their adventurous and rebellious spirit. Like the Monkey King, these traits of boldness and defiance were to stand us in good stead to face the racism of the times and grapple with the melting pot myth. We were trying to make a living, to survive in the Chinese hand laundries, and submit to the trials to which we were presented. My parents were limited by their inability to speak English and the absence of economic opportunities in this land of freedom. The sociopolitical contexts, and the day-by-day living in a bicultural environment created a harsh reality. We needed the immigration legends—the stories of wealth that we created for families back home, the dreams of returning to an idyllic China—to weather the tests of survival and trials of endurance to combat racism and poverty.

In *Journey to the West,* Monkey King and all his companions are transformed as they travel through their fantastic adventures. The Toisanese immigrants traveled East to get to the West; as they immigrated to the shores of *Fa Kay* (Flowered Flag) or *Mei Kuo* (Beautiful Country), as America was called, they too needed to accomplish their 81 deeds. Their journey was captured in the letters sent to families in China—storytelling. These stories described the unimaginable: gold in the streets, riches of Westerners, and luxurious living. These stories were made believable by the money that accompanied these letters to starving families in Guangzhou, China. Women and children with husbands and fathers in *gnoy yerng* (overseas) bragged about and enjoyed the material comforts provided by their husbands and fathers.

After the letter writing, the Chinese immigrant men would congregate in their family clan associations in Mei Kuo with other stories—stories of racism, Chinatowns burning, working the dust of gold mines long abandoned by the white men, cleaning the dirty laundry of the bak gui (white devils), and bearing the brunt of racist behavior. On Sundays, the only non-working day, stories abound of how the *bak gui* will never let you forget that your skin is yellow, and how the land of equal opportunity was only open to whites. They shared stories of starvation here in America, of having to sleep on hard ironing boards instead of beds, of toiling in the laundry 12 hours a day and 6 days a week with little rest. They shared their dreams of returning home to China to retire as rich men. Their enlightenment was but a vision; their transformation a dream. They reminisced and dreamed of the endless beauty of China, a place where lychee nuts grew in abundance and fell off the trees to be picked; a place where they would be honored for being old. Out of these stories grew the immigration myths—a mix of truth and embellishment.

Rethinking the Past

As we look back, there are the stories of regret and remorse. I remember stories about Ah Sam Gung (Number Three Great Uncle) who slaved away for 40 years selling 10-cent cups of coffee and one-dollar meals; he always managed to send money back to his wife in China while living under squalid conditions in America. Believing that Ah Sam Gung was a rich man in America (since he never corrected this myth), his wife treated her friends and relatives in China to generous banquets and gifts. Left by her husband as a young bride in her 20s, she joined him as an elderly woman in her 60s in the United States; she lived the remaining 15 years of her life in misery, crying and chastising herself for her spendthrift ways while she now lived in near-poverty conditions. She cried daily over how she and her husband had lost the best years of their lives apart.

Another uncle, Ah Suk, came to America on his own at the age of 15. He found work to support himself, built a restaurant business, and raised a family; but he never saw his parents again, a fact he bemoaned. He could not bring himself to talk about this even as a grandparent, as it brought back such intense feelings of pain and loss. As I listened to these stories, I turned to look at my son, then 14, unable to imagine his making it in another country on his own without family support, or to bear the thought of my never seeing him again for the rest of my life.

The misunderstandings between generations and in relationships are enhanced by the themes of immigration. I saw the escalation of father-son conflict as my brother reached adolescence. Bound by expectations of parental obligation that he could not meet, he withdrew by staying out late to avoid conflict—not out of fear, but out of respect. Angry and helpless by what he perceived as disrespect and disobedience, my father locked him out.

My mother was able to change with the times. While she did not understand the fashion or the music of the times, she was always one to be amused and tolerant. She would drop her chin and roll her eyes, feigning shock at the rising prices of objects and remind us when a loaf of bread was only 5 cents. She would laugh and shake her head in disbelief at the new fashions that featured torn and faded jeans. Once my nephew was wearing wrinkled clothes—the fashion of the day. Having done his laundry one evening, he stuffed his clothes into a basket to get the perfect set of wrinkles. My mother noticed how wrinkled they were; from her days as a laundrywoman, she "took pity" on him and ironed all his shirts smooth. Ever the respectful grandchild, my nephew dared not correct her. When my mother found the clothes she had neatly ironed wrinkled up back in the basket, she was confused. She shook her head in disbelief when I explained that this was the fashion.

With only a sixth-grade education, my mother was a prolific letter writer, although she was self-conscious that her writing was not scholarly enough. She relied on the *Hung Yeem Do Ann* (dictionary of homonyms) to find the same sounding radicals she needed to understand a word's meaning and find the right word. As I started graduate school, I began to appreciate her issues from a psychological perspective. Or perhaps it was my journey through life with my mother at my side that helped me to rethink my culture and my identity. As I rethought the past and met our ancestors in the present, there were paradoxes and contradictions to reconcile. My mother and I expanded our emotional and cultural bonds.

I begin to think of the stories my mother told and retold. Now I hear them differently and look at my mother in a new light. Where I saw dependency before, I now saw her bold and fierce spirit. Where I felt annoyance and impatience, I now appreciate her plight of leaving her home, family, and culture. Where I saw contradiction in her obedience to my father versus her challenging of society, I now see them reconciled. In writing her story, I seek to create her immigration legend, and to preserve her voice for our children and grandchildren to form our bonds together.

Part III

TRANSFORMATION AND ENLIGHTENMENT

With regard to the Chinese immigrant experience, two images stand out: the journey to the West made by Chinese immigrant families and the women warriors as Chinese immigrant women fight the battles against racism, poverty, trauma, and loss. The journey of immigration has many challenges; immigrants face many trials that test their resolve. They become warriors on a sojourn to return to their true identities; they become transformed and enlightened in the process.

For Chinese immigrants, their true identities may not be integrated; rather, a Chinese American identity may be separated—that is, bicultural, both Chinese and American—much like an egg—the yolk from the albumin, the yin from the yang. The developmental task is not acculturation to a Western way of life, but biculturalism toward a new identity amidst the contradictions and paradoxes of both Asian and Western ways.

Sometimes the myths and stories get lost as second- and third-generation immigrant families travel through the ages; they lose their culture and their identities. Often each generation seeks to reconnect with their roots and ancestry as they make this journey. Often, it is women's connectedness that provides the bonds for immigrant families to preserve and enhance their family and cultural mythologies.

It is in their stories that intergenerational bonds are created. At the same time, the psychological bondage often hovers over preventing us from escaping the confines of our minds or the boundaries of our cultures. As the journey continues, each family draws on the stories in its family and cultural histories to create its own immigration legend.

As Monkey King journeyed to the Jade Mountain in the west in search of enlightenment, our Western sisters and brothers journeyed to the Garden of Eden in the east in search of knowledge. Early American pioneers were westward bound, while Chinese immigrants were eastward bound in search of the Golden Mountains of the west.

Part III ends with an attempt to integrate mythology and story-telling into the immigration story. While the family saga in this book is uniquely Chinese American, all immigrant families must grapple with the neverending themes of immigration. As our society becomes increasingly multicultural, counselors working with immigrant families must grapple with these themes and develop the multicultural compe-tencies to be effective. The lessons in Chapter 8 are intended to do that, as well as to suggest what immigrant families must do to heal, to grow, and to bond. Immigrant families must leave a legacy for their children and grandchildren—that is, they must create immigration legend.

CHAPTER 7

Of Bonds and Bondage

As Time Goes By

Today, in the land we call America, I stand tall,
As part of the second generation to carry on our heritage.
Listening to so many stories
And learning the true meaning of survival,
I was fascinated and enthralled.
My responsibility to my family in continuing customary practices
Will be a dedication I pledge.
As our beliefs and values get passed from generation to generation,
The unity we form will truly be what a family stands for.
We will represent one, like a confederation,
With lineage serving as the core.
In accord with tradition, I will help to hand down history
And charm that's harmonized in combination,
Because I know that my ancestors would be filled with pride
And they deserve our admiration.

Tracey Lynette Ong

IDENTITY AND BONDING .

As contrasting values in Chinese and Western cultures compete with each other, Chinese immigrant families need to embrace a bicultural approach to their identity formation. This means splitting aspects of one's identity where disparate parts cannot be integrated. In clinging to trauma and loss brought about by the immigration experience, immigrant families can remain sheltered and unable to escape the narrow confines of ethnic Chinatowns. The bonds and bondage of culture infuse themselves into the day-by-day living of all immigrant families.

CHINESE AMERICAN IDENTITY

What is a Chinese American? I always knew I was Chinese for as long as I could remember. My parents and all who met me ingrained it in me. The first question I was always asked was, "Are Chinese or Japanese?" I would always answer "Chinese" before we could go on. Not until I traveled to Europe as an adult did I come to the jolting realization that I was also American. This was the era of the "Ugly American," known for vulgarity in dress and manners, uninitiated into the more refined customs of European culture, and accustomed to the excesses of material spending with newfound wealth. While going through customs on a highway in Germany, the officer, never having seen an Asian face before, asked me the usual question with a smile: "Chinois?" or Chinese, to which I promptly replied, "Yes" as I always have. Much to my surprise, he was outraged, upon looking at my passport, that I would be so audacious as to try to pass myself off as Chinese when, "You're an American!"

Racism and our sociopolitical context were realities that coerced us to think, "Who am I?" as we grew up in America. The melting pot myth said we would all blend together. Yet the daily questioning prevented us from blending into the great American melting pot. The melting pot was a symbol created to give meaning to and instill patriotism in European white immigrants; it had little meaning for most Chinese immigrants, since they were not allowed to partake as full citizens in mainstream society.

One of the earliest models of Chinese American identity was developed by Sue and Sue (1971); it was a trait model characterizing the traditional, marginal, and Asian American man. Acculturation to American culture was at the core of these models reflected in unidimensional assessments, which presume that Asians become more Westernized over time.

It has become clear that models of identity development need to be multidimensional or bidimensional to recognize bidirectionality of the process and independent identification with native and host cultures. There has also been a shift from static to dynamic process models; J. Kim

(1981) identifies five stages of identity development, including ethnic awareness, white identification, awakening to social political consciousness, redirection (reconnection), and incorporation. The incorporation stage represents the highest form of identity evolution, encompassing a positive and comfortable identity.

For Asian Americans, ethnicity is typically more prominent than race in defining identity; immigration plays a significant role in the evolution of cultural identity; and biculturalism is integral, reflecting the influence of two contrasting cultures.

The Family Reunification Act of 1965 enabled Chinese immigrant men in the United States to be reunited with their families in China. As this happened, we learned that we had established a new culture here in the United States that was uniquely Chinese American, although our parents and society had insisted we were Chinese. We began to learn that Chinese Americans needed to split our identities in order to remain whole. East and West sometimes simply could not meet; these were the ironies of biculturalism.

Cultural Bonds, Cultural Bondage

Cultural myths and symbols have helped immigrant families to create a common bond while also keeping them in lifelong bondage. The journey of immigration has resulted in feelings of helplessness and hopelessness as immigrant families face the oppression of racism, the clash of cultures, and the subordination of women.

The bondage of culture is not unlike foot binding, a practice begun in the Sung dynasty (960–976 BC), reportedly to imitate an imperial concubine who was required to dance with her feet bound. By the 12th century, the practice was widespread until the establishment of the Republic of China in 1911. Chinese women with small feet were considered beautiful; therefore, girls had their feet bound to maintain their small size. With the constriction of natural growth, the feet became deformed and women were unable to walk. Bound feet symbolize the bondage imposed upon Chinese women in distorted values about feminine beauty.

Confucian values, which created a male-dominanted society in China, did not prevent Chinese immigrant women from taking prominent roles in creating the cultural bonds to sustain the family and Chinese American identity. As Chinese immigrant women arrived to join their bachelor husbands, they recreated the home, family, and communities that they had left behind. As racism pervaded American society and communism overtook Chinese society, Chinese American immigrants became more secretive for fear of being deported and communities became more insular in protecting Chinese culture. The white mainstream society colluded with immigrant communities to make Chinese Americans exotic and create atmospheres of mistrust. My parents were so fearful that they would be deemed communists by distrustful whites that they disposed of their Chinese newspapers by burning them.

This sociopolitical milieu contributed to anti-Asian legislative policies, social attitudes, and behaviors. There was many a dinner table conversation when my father, after his evening dinner drink of scotch, would begin his tirade about the ineptness of the current American government. While his criticism was intense, he never felt he had the power to change it. As children, we would become impatient. "Go back to China," we would say. We were more optimistic; believing we were the promise of our parents' pilgrimage to the West, we believed we could change anything.

We grew up in America under the "melting pot" myth; soon this became a "salad bowl" image as society struggled with racial and cultural differences that would not blend over time. As adults, we came to see society value and savor the distinct cultures and their unique characteristics. The social climate underwent radical changes during the civil rights and women's movements of the 1960s and 1970s, which advocated for social change and racial equity. The shift in ideology from the cultural paranoia of our childhood to the valuing of differences created new symbols of peace and antiwar fervor that prevailed in U.S. society in our adulthood. John F. Kennedy gave us renewed hope of a new society and promised that all was possible.

A Mother's Pride

Although my mother believed in education, graduations simply did not seem important, because it was an American custom. Although she supported our education and was always proud of our accomplishments, she refused to participate in any school functions or parent events because of her inability to speak English. Her excuse was always, "I don't understand what they're saying; I'd just sit there like an idiot or a crazy person."

When I published my first book, I gave my mother a copy, knowing full well she would not be able to read it. She looked at me puzzled, and as always, protested that she could not read English; she said, "What was the point?" I felt foolish until I shared this story with my coauthor. He had done the same with his mother who spoke only Spanish; he told me how he had given the book to his mother, and before she could protest, simply told her to keep it on her coffee table for company. We both knew the importance of having our mother's pride behind our accomplishments. And though our mothers could not read English and could not always comprehend the nature of our accomplishments, their pride and pleasure were always communicated through the simple gesture of showing off our accomplishments to friends and family. These were the images that sustained us.

POVERTY AMIDST PLENTY

America was the land of plenty, or so we were told. We read the schoolbooks that we thought mirrored what Americans looked like. Only it did not look like the urban America in which we lived. The white characters of Dick and Jane in towns where everyone lived in a "white house with a picket fence" and every child had a room of their own just didn't look like our homes. These images existed only in the storybooks.

Survival in America

We lived in a small four-room railroad apartment and were told how lucky we were that we were not living in the back of the laundry. My brother, sister, and I shared the largest room—the parlor—while my parents took the bedroom; there remained the kitchen and a 10-by-9-foot living room. We had one chest of drawers for all the family's clothes; each of us had our own drawer. Mine was the smallest since I was the youngest in the family. We all shared one closet, so many of our possessions needed to be stacked at the foot of the beds. When my parents finally got their own chest of drawers, we were so excited because now we could all have another drawer. How we envied Dick and Jane in the storybooks, and what we saw among our white friends.

We kept a clean apartment, but that did not stop the roaches. Our neighborhood was old and in the city. Despite repeating spraying, the roaches were hardy; I guess they too needed to survive in these dismal circumstances. The light switch to the apartment was in the middle of the room. When we entered the apartment at night, we would have to walk halfway into a dark room to open the light. (Note my translation from Chinese; it was not until I was an adult that my son called my attention to the fact that you *turn on* a light.) We were always ready for those roaches. As soon as we opened the light, the roaches would scatter, and we would stomp on hundreds of roaches. This was poverty, only we didn't know it.

There was no privacy in these railroad apartments. We closed one entrance to create more privacy; still, you could see straight into every room from the kitchen entrance. Our bedroom had the only window looking out to the front so my parents would enter the room whenever they wanted to look out the window. As teenagers, my sister and I would change behind the closet door or hide in the bathroom, the only room in the apartment with a lock. It was not until my brother went away to college that my sister conspired with me to create our own room. We moved his belongings into the living room and left him the open-up couch as his bed when he came home.

We rarely ate out at restaurants because it was considered too expensive. On those rare occasions, my father would order one order of Kwangtung Chow Mein for the entire family. We could never buy the things we wanted because they were always too expensive. As we struggled with not having enough, never being able to afford to eat in restaurants, never having the clothes that our American peers wore, always having to count our money and ask the price before we bought something, we wondered if this was indeed the land of freedom and opportunity.

Despite the poverty, my mother created a home and a culture for us in Brooklyn during a time when few Chinese women had immigrated to America. As the economy became worse and our laundry business declined, there was not enough to make ends meet. My parents' pride prevented them from asking for handouts. My mother began "bootlegging" to supplement the laundry business income. She would brew a rice wine at home once a month. These would be bottled into gallon jugs and sold to relatives and friends to make an extra buck. Having no car for transportation, we would carry these gallon jugs two at a time on the subways for delivery. We were urged to be very secretive about this out of fear that we would be arrested. But I remember how my mother would beam with pride when she delivered one of these gallon jugs of wine to an eager customer; her humility would not allow her to brag, but her face waited with anticipation for the compliment.

Money was ever so important as a measure of prosperity; thus, Toisanese Chinese will feel no qualms about asking you how much you make, or how much something costs. When my father came to visit me in my new house in the suburbs, he wandered through the house mumbling, "rich man's house." Given his Chinese pride, he could not share the pride he felt at our accomplishment nor the discomfort he felt at being out of place in his daughter's home. Having lived a life of struggle and poverty, he could not reconcile himself to the comforts of middle-class living. He always remained poor in his mind.

Remembering the Poverty in China

As children, we could never understand why my parents emphasized some things all the time. "You must serve a chicken to celebrate someone's birthday." "Don't show your true feelings because they will take advantage of you." "You must study and work hard." These admonitions were constant and repetitive. Sometimes we became irritated. Other times, we simply ignored them. We were always reminded to finish our rice because of all the people starving in China as well as the beggars in the streets. We would impatiently and jokingly tell my mother to send it back to them. My mother often told pitiful stories of women who were so poor that they could not produce breast milk to nurse their starving children, or how a family of four had to share one bowl of rice for dinner.

The stories of poverty told by my mother never generated the sympathy from us that she had wanted them to. As Chinese Americans, we were arrogant; we could not know poverty and starvation because we never went without a meal. Only as an adult could I realize how my parents' experiences of poverty and starvation back in China shaped their worldviews forever—how they felt compelled to make these admonitions in the continuing fear that they might experience such hardships once again.

Forever influenced by her past experiences of starvation and as a good Chinese mother, my mother would save the best pieces of food for us while she ate the worst during any meal we would have together. This was a mother's love; in this way, she could show how much she cared and sacrificed for us. My mother was always generous with others and frugal with herself. She believed this was one of the highest virtues she could achieve as a woman.

In our adult years as our economic circumstances improved, my mother could never give up her thrifty mentality. When shopping with us at a mall, she would always widen her eyes in amazement at the high cost of things. For herself, she would wear rags and mend things well beyond their useful life (by our standards). Though she was appreciative of our gifts to honor her, she kept many of them unused for years; ultimately, she would give them away because they were too good for her to use.

In spite of my mother's thriftiness, she insisted on maintaining our pride. We were taught never to show that we were wanting. We needed to carry our heads up high (following her years of taunting by village children). Yet she could not comprehend the same rules in American society. Since she often tried to make do with what we had, clothes used only for one occasion was not a priority. I recall my sister's sixth-grade graduation; everyone was to wear a white dress. My mother would not, or could not, afford a white dress for my sister. Instead, she found a dress that had been washed so much that all the color had come off. My mother felt this was adequate enough for one occasion and made my sister wear it, to her great distress and humiliation.

An Awakening of Asian Pride

Chinatown in the 1960s and 1970s showed an awakening of Asian pride. The leaders were younger men and women in their 20s and 30s, many aligned with the civil rights movement and the Asian American movement; they showed a force of strength as they created Chinatown's social welfare programs. Soon there were factions competing for community control. Younger groups challenged the long-standing power of the Chinese Consolidated Benevolent Association, made up of Chinese elders from all the family clan associations and historically known as the power base of Chinatown.

There was now a new middle class of Chinese Americans. Families from Hong Kong immigrated to join their families in New York. Second-generation *jook sing* (American-born Chinese) were now adults. A new Asian American culture was born. Having grown up in an urban environment, they dressed fashionably in Western garb and stood out in stark contrast to the old-timers—the elderly Chinese women with knitted hats, layers of sweaters, and *men knop* (Chinese-style down-filled vests) or the elderly Chinese men with their white shirts, buttoned cardigan sweaters and caps, always smoking a cigarette. These newer immigrants filled the streets of New York's Chinatown. The number of street peddlers who sold vegetables and trinkets at unbeatable prices multiplied; they could do so because they had no overhead and only wanted to survive.

Suddenly there were Asian youth gangs with origins in Hong Kong that terrorized the community. Family clan associations seeking to gain control of Chinatown often supported these gangs to protect their economic and business interests in the form of the many gambling houses that they owned. The Flying Dragons, the gang supported by the Hip Sing clan association, "owned Pell Street" (Kinkead, 1991); the Ghost Shadows, the gang supported by the On Leong clan association, "owned" Mott Street. The gangs were the muscle for the Chinese elders to collect debts and extortion money. Suddenly we had Chinese preying on Chinese, extorting Chinatown businesses for protection money; Chinatown was no longer the safe haven.

Confucius Plaza: The End of an Era

In front of Confucius Plaza, a publicly funded housing project with mixed income housing, where my mother lived during the last 2 decades of her life, stands a 10-foot bronze statue of the sage Confucius. This was a present from the Chinese Consolidated Benevolent Association. It is a different era now. Cher Long Foong, the Lau clan association, is now defunct. My father has passed away, as have many of the elder men of his generation. Families moved away. Few were willing to pay the fee to maintain this association since they were no longer congregating there on their day off. Most men had families now. These small family clan associations are largely gone; in their place are the social service agencies.

Many more elderly women now congregate at the associations created by the social welfare programs, or at the Mulberry Street Park on sunny, warm days. My mother used to hang out there as she had done decades earlier at the clan association. These women now exchange stories of the hardships in the garment factories that have since replaced the laundries. These "sweatshops" provide a sewing machine and a chair; women work piecework in a production line, getting a few cents a seam; many would need to work 12-hour days to make $200 per week. There is no minimum wage and minimal protection from safety hazards. The lowest paid workers, mostly women in their 60s and 70s, no longer as swift or as skilled, were the thread cutters; they snip threads from finished garments and are paid pennies per garment.

The younger women with children often cannot afford babysitters and have to leave their children home alone after school. I remember the stories of my Poy Kim's (Maternal Aunt's) niece, who talked of playing in the stairwell landing outside the garment factory after school while waiting for her mother to finish work. There were no toys; at one point, they played in a large box discarded from a garment delivery. Life in America was supposed to have been the better life, but we see these families in bondage, imprisoned by the economic realities of our society.

Power of the Unspoken Word

There are issues within Chinese families that are never spoken about. There were things we always knew and felt. As my mother would say, "You should not have to be told!" We knew our parents expected us to respect them. We knew how important it was to be Chinese. We knew the importance of family. Perhaps it was the way my parents looked or in the sternness with which they spoke. We might boldly say in defiance that we had a choice not to do something in order to demonstrate that we had minds of our own, especially in adolescence when we believed we knew everything. However, we knew deep down that there were things we could never do because of the power of the unspoken word. We simply did not challenge them.

When cultural taboo did not permit something, nonverbal and somatic symptoms expressed the unspoken. The stress of poverty and immigration manifested itself in somatic symptoms in both my parents. I remember a period in my mother's life when she began to develop many physical and somatic ailments as she tried to cope with the hardships in her life. She would threaten suicide, in typical Chinese fashion and exasperation. We usually felt it was a means of controlling us. She would threaten to jump off the Brooklyn Bridge, but would wait for the next milestone in our lives (e.g., to see us married, to see us graduate). At another point, she developed bleeding ulcers, which were life threatening, from her years of sacrifice and internalizing her distress. Having to endure poverty, leaving behind her eldest son, and not being there for her father's death were stress inducers; most of all, she was angry over my father's domineering personality and bad temper, but felt that a dutiful and virtuous wife should not complain. According to Chinese tradition, sacrifice was to have its rewards; my mother was becoming disenchanted. Her illnesses and threats were her ways of telling us this.

My father was a proud man. Despite his violent temper, he was unable to speak about his vulnerabilities. His periodic outbreaks of dermatitis spoke for him. Compelled to fulfill his provider and protector roles as father and husband, these outbreaks of dermatitis provided the means of relief. My father became more volatile and more rigid in his ways; he vented his frustrations on my mother as he felt more trapped by the absence of choices before him. Although having a bad temper is not a valued trait in Chinese culture, it is sanctioned as part of a man's character. He resorted to smoking and alcohol as two vices that helped to numb the pain. He smoked at least a pack a day, and insisted on a shot of whiskey with his dinner. He developed emphysema in his later years, which consumed most of his lungs; yet he boldly refused to give up "his only two enjoyments in life."

The New Role of Women

As U.S. society began to question the roles of women through the women's movement, Chinese Americans also questioned the Chinese cultural tradition about the honored role of men. We questioned whether a marriage should be premised on the subservience of women to men. We became annoyed with my mother's subservience to my father's needs. We would get angry about her constant sacrifice at the cost of her own needs. We would get angry that she would put others before herself. We would urge her to stand up for herself. We could not understand how difficult it was for her to transcend the Chinese belief about a woman's honor—that is, to be moral and virtuous, not to be selfish, but to be generous and nurturing so that others will shower you with respect and gifts.

A defining moment during my childhood, however, demonstrated how bold my mother could be in her own way. As my parents walked together on their way home from Chinatown, my father turned to her and chided, "Don't walk so close to me, it doesn't look nice!" He was expecting my mother to walk 10 paces behind him; women were expected to do so in China as a sign of deference to their husbands. I saw my mother get furious and stand up for herself, saying, "I'm your wife! I'm not a prostitute! What do you mean it doesn't look nice?" Though known for his violent temper, my father did not protest. For a moment, he must have forgotten that times had changed; he was no longer in China during those good old days. He was aware that he too needed to adjust to different ideas about the roles of men and women.

FREEDOM: LEARNING FROM MY MOTHER'S VOICE

What do we learn from this journey of immigration? The context has changed but the stories remain the same. Chinese immigrant women have been women warriors, fighting undercover against the injustices of racism, gender bias, and poverty in a man's world. My mother found freedom in the new roles for women that society supported in the 1960s.

Having Face

It was through our eyes, her children, that my mother saw America. Since she spoke little English, we translated for her and escorted her to places other than Chinatown. Like most Chinese immigrants, her fear of mainstream society was pervasive.

As she viewed America through our eyes, we viewed China through hers. She would sing the praises of Chinese culture—a culture of thousands of years compared to the American culture of only a few hundred years. She would describe the splendor of Chinese artifacts and the advances of Chinese technology. I became interested in the abacus that she used to compute the laundry prices; I would watch her use this rack of beads to rapidly compute complex arithmetic simply by moving the beads. She taught me the practice exercise accompanied by a song used as a pneumonic device for addition and subtraction; it is not unlike the alphabet song familiar to most American children.

Through these times, we learned the importance of "having face," a trait so valued in Asian culture that it becomes paramount in many interactions. This means showing respect for others and maintaining the dignity of ourselves. Since most immigrants experienced starvation prior to coming to the United States, the abundance of food is highly significant. Though we were frugal on a daily basis, we were always sure to have excess food whenever guests were invited to dinner. This was intended to demonstrate respect and honor of our guests, and to maintain our dignity by showing our plentiful resources. Some Toisanese immigrant families will insist on having their own meal at home before joining another family at their home for a holiday dinner; this was intended to avoid the risk of being considered beggars or ridiculed for not being able to afford their own food.

As children, we viewed all these practices with some disdain and bewilderment. We understood the pride, but some of these practices no longer served a useful purpose. In America where food was in abundance, Chinese immigrants held strongly to practices that didn't make sense out of their original context.

One defining moment of the importance of Asian pride stands out in my mind. A neighborhood parent had come to my mother to complain about my behavior after her daughter and I had had a fight; I have long forgotten the reason for that fight. All I remember was my mother slapping me across my face upon hearing the neighbor's complaint, to my dismay, shame, and anger. Even the neighbor was embarrassed and quickly suggested that it was all right. After the neighbor left, my mother explained to me that she did not think I was wrong; but she did not want the neighbor to think that she had not done a good job as a parent in disciplining me. She did not want to "lose face."

Children Are Like Birds

My mother would often become pensive and sad, and say: "Children are like birds; they grow up and fly away!" During these times, there was little that could be said to dissuade her. We were always too quick to dismiss her musings, especially when our contrasting views led to disagreement and frustration. My mother would then say, "Just wait until you become a parent, you'll see." These memories and my mother's words were mirrors to the future.

We Shall Not Forget

As my mother aged, she tended to her plants and picked up knitting to pass the time when she was not visiting with friends and relatives or exercising. She knitted hats galore with the signature quality of so many of her contemporaries. She was always proud of her creations, giving them as gifts to friends, relatives, and us in her continuing efforts to nurture and demonstrate her generosity.

She had come a long way from the days when her ulcers and somatic symptoms symbolized her powerlessness and anger. She had accomplished her work of raising her children, and remained proud. When we did not travel, my mother would visit me in Massachusetts. She would never stay long for fear of intruding; she fought to maintain her independence and refused to live with any one of her children, which is contrary to Chinese tradition. She continued her nurturing roles in mending our clothes, cooking up special dishes, or cleaning and organizing my kitchen while I was at work. My mother often brought with her "care packages"—Chinese dry foods and herbal tonic ingredients that she thought I did not know about or have time to buy. She would carefully label each product and write down the instructions for using them in Chinese. It was as if she intended to ensure that these special recipes for herbal tonics would be passed on for posterity.

My mother had dreams that paralleled the idealism of the civil rights movement and women's movement of the 1960s. These were times of great transformation in the fight for freedom, and the images of that era are embodied in my mother's words. I hear her voice and her wisdom as loudly as the day they were spoken; they soothe and guide my actions. I am constantly reminded of her stories, and her heeding that "We shall not forget" the suffering, the pain, and the challenges of those who came before.

CHAPTER 8

Of Intergenerational Bonds: Lessons

Take on the World

Each day is filled with love and hate,
Surviving it all leads us to our uncontrollable fate.
Being lost in our own unforeseen tunnel,
We seem like we're always on our defense,
Despite the love and anger,
We can take on the world no matter how intense,
Ready for whatever our future holds for us,
Whether good or bad, we'll do what we must.

Tracey Lynette Ong

Through storytelling, we all develop our family sagas and create immigration legends. These legends are carried through the generations and connect us. Whether it is the story of the Pilgrims arriving on the eastern shores of Plymouth or the Chinese arriving on the western shores of San Francisco, immigrants share a common legend. The loss and abandonment of people and things are endured by immigrants in order to start anew, in their quest on the journey to the west. All immigrants are pioneers in search of enlightenment and the good life. All immigrants cope with the ghosts in our past and present, that is, the "isms" of class, race, gender, and age. All transform themselves in the process and become bicultural beings. Often, the myths with which they live put them in bondage that restricts and limits them from partaking in the

142

new world; some immigrants end up in ghettos smaller and more insular than the places they left, living in squalid economic conditions even when social and financial means no longer limit their options.

On this journey, there are visions from our images and memories, messages from our voices. They are both negative and positive—our bonds and bondage. The media, our society, and environment often reinforce the negative messages that entrap us, perpetuate the ghosts that haunt us, and put us in bondage. We must create the legends and the stories to capture these intergenerational bonds, to give us voice. We must create more powerful images to free us, to connect with the power within, and to participate in the process of transformation.

COUNSELING CHINESE AMERICAN IMMIGRANT FAMILIES: IMPLICATIONS

This book is a celebration of women, of families, and of culture as the sustaining forces that guide us along the journey of life and of immigration. As we examine mythology and legend, saga and symbols to understand the plight of Chinese immigrants, there are lessons to be learned that we can model for future generations of immigrants. This book is a journey toward understanding the psyche of Chinese Americans.

Culture Matters!

To counsel Chinese American immigrant families, counselors must understand this journey. The differences between Asian and Western cultures are to be valued; the various cultural myths and legends are to be understood. These differences tell us about our clients. More importantly, this book illustrates the use of storytelling as a method for counselors when working with immigrant families. In telling their story, families can heal from the trauma of the immigration experience. Counselors can help families in this healing process if they can view the immigration experience through the lens of their clients. The intergenerational bonds felt by immigrant families can transmit pathological or healthy influences if only counselors can know what to pull from their stories. In using storytelling as a method, counselors can help clients to change outcomes that victimize and oppress to ones that promote growth and healing. Counselors should help immigrant families understand, remember, and relive the family saga about how they came to the United States. Storytelling as a technique facilitates the expression of affect and the resolution of conflict.

Multicultural competencies (Sue & Carter, 1998) have been widely embraced by professional counseling and psychology; they developed a three characteristic by three dimension matrix of beliefs/attitudes, knowledge, and skills, which interact with counselor awareness of their own values and biases, counselor awareness of clients' worldviews, and culturally appropriate intervention strategies, resulting in a total of 31 multicultural counseling competencies.

This matrix can be applied to counselors working with immigrant families. Counselors need to move from an intrapersonal perspective to an interpersonal one to make use of the contexts in which immigrants and their families are embedded. Counselors must learn to use cultural symbols important to clients since these can be valuable in communicating a therapeutic message. They should draw on cultural mythology because these stories tell what is important to a culture and to families. Most of all, counselors can help immigrant families to create their own immigration legends and create bonding images. These are the stories of dilemma, loss, escape, hope, and challenge that all immigrants face.

These principles are summarized in lessons for working with immigrant families. They identify the bondage messages, bonding image, and the action steps to be taken with a discussion of the principle. The prescriptive format is consistent with the emphasis on the authority as mentor, while the bonding image draws on cultural metaphor as a tool for teaching. Creating immigration legend is a process. As Monkey King so aptly puts it, he can leap a thousand *li* (miles) to get to where he wants to in a second, but he must travel on foot to reach his destiny in 16 years; the developmental process cannot be rushed. The journey and the creation of legend is a process.

REINFORCE THE TWO FACES OF WOMAN

The first two lessons are about our notions of women. Stereotypes, culture, and gender expectations have prescribed roles for women that have been limited. The two lessons recommend that counselors work to reinforce the two faces of women in our images of them as women warrior and moon goddesses.

Lesson 1. Warrior Lessons: Celebrate Strength

Bondage Message: Women need to be rescued; women are cunning and manipulative beings whose power must be feared.
Bonding Image: The woman warrior.

Action: Celebrate strength and pride. We cannot use our swords against the ghosts of our past. We need to see the barricades of racism and stereotypes, which block and silence us. With words as her sword and power in her voice, a woman can fight to connect with her power from within.

Principle

The woman warrior in literature, both the classic and contemporary versions, celebrates women's strengths as they face challenges in a paradoxical world. My mother was that woman warrior. Her story connects with all the women who fight the battle against images and expectations that put them in bondage—a mother who defies images of the subservient, passive Chinese American female, yet is bound by them. Her story, like that of the woman warrior, is about a Chinese American woman's attempt to find a uniquely Chinese American voice.

The bondage is the battle we must fight; as women warriors face the challenges, find new strength, and create the bonds, we find there can be new beginnings that transform our Chinese American identity. The bondage of contemporary Asian American women is having to think about fitting in, having to fight being stereotyped as exotic and delicate. Gender roles put women into bondage when they expect men and boys to be fighters and women and girls to be rescued; hence the dilemma of the woman warrior and the outcome of most classic Western fairy tales.

Warrior Lessons (Eng, 1999) picks up from *The Woman Warrior;* whereas the latter gives Asian American women a voice, the former attempts to provide answers (i.e., lessons) about how Asian American women can search for strength and identity—it is a transformative process and a journey. The contemporary Asian American woman must confront the "isms" of the present and the ghosts of the past to reach the enlightenment of the future. To preserve and maintain one's culture of origin without being devalued as traditional, to challenge the racism in present-day society without being marginalized as pathological, to live one's identity to the fullest—these are the goals of the contemporary woman warrior. The fight against stereotypes and being held to a higher standard are the lessons to be learned; we need to end with admiration, not pity.

Contrasting Images of Women

Chinese history and legend celebrate women of great character whose attempts to fulfill responsibilities involved significant conflict, sacrifice, and determination (Yu, 1974a, 1974b). Typically, favorable images portray women who achieve power and fame through their cleverness, responsibility, or prowess; in the end, they reunite with their families of origin as the final test of maturity, as in Hua Muk Lan. Several contrasting images of women follow.

Rescue Fantasy Versus Woman Warrior. Woman warrior images, compared to Madame Butterfly images, celebrate the journey, accomplishment, and transformation of Hua Muk Lan, who became a famous warrior in the guise of a man. For Chinese American immigrant women, the woman warrior image celebrates the ability of women to fight the battle against images and expectations that put them in bondage.

Asian Dolls: Subservience Versus Pride. Images of Asian women as subservient portray them as fragile toys and exotic objects. They reflect a superficial interpretation of Confucian values that limits and restricts the range of roles for Asian women. They need to be replaced with those that celebrate a women's pride.

A Woman's Honor and Virtue. "To die with honor is better than to live with shame" is a motto in Chinese Confucian society. While avoidance of shame is important in Asian cultures, the options a woman had in Confucian society were limited and dependent on men. Western stories distort these images to the benefit of white men, while misinterpretation of Asian images suggest weakness and pathology. Reconstruction of a woman's honor and virtue through independence and choice for Chinese American immigrant women are needed to empower and free them.

Lesson 2. Woman's Connectedness

Bondage Message: Women are meek, subservient, and victimized.
Bonding Image: The fertilizing power of the Moon Goddess.
Action: Draw on the connectedness of femalehood and nurturing aspects of motherhood to form family and intergenerational bonds.

Principle

Through the ages, it has been women's connectedness that created the spirit, provided the strength, and nurtured the bonds that hold families together. The veneration for the mother and the fertilizing power of women is embodied in images of moon goddesses in mythology.

Mothers in Asian mythology are powerful, benevolent, forgiving, nurturing mentors. Chinese immigrant women can embrace these positive images as they nurture, feed, and heal their families.

EXPAND OUR NOTIONS OF FAMILY

Counselors working with Chinese American immigrants must recognize the importance of the extended family within Chinese culture as well as the hierarchical relationship between family members.

Lesson 3. Of Intergenerational Bonds

Bondage Message: Our family "ghosts" will haunt us forever and cannot be changed.
Bonding Image: The harmony of the Chinese banquet.
Action: Promote family and intergenerational bonds.

Principle

As immigrant families assimilate into a new culture, their extended family relationships and intergenerational bonds can nurture and sustain them in their journey. They must avoid the bondage of cultural myths that limit their opportunities and stereotype their roles. There must be a balance and harmony in these relationships, as in the perfect Chinese banquet, where the whole is greater than the sum of its parts.

Gender and Family Roles. Asian mythology describe gender and family roles in relationship to one another; male and female, elder and younger are related, as in the yin-yang balance of the universe; they are interdependent; they cannot be independent of one another. These contrast with Western images of the battle of the sexes, the conquering of parental figures, or jealousy between women.

Mother–Son: Obligation. While mythology portrays the journey of separation-individuation or independence from parents in stories of mother–son relationships, the importance of a son's loyalty and obligation to the family is primary, as is a mother's influence over her son.

Mother–Daughter: Bonding. Mothers and daughters share an emotional bond that can transcend generational differences based on women's connectedness. Together they can create the immigration legend that transforms the future. As in *The Joy Luck Club,* the journey may be one of initial disdain and rebelliousness against maternal expectations; the transformation is when daughters come to realize how perceptive their mothers are and come to value what they have gained. The process is in establishing their mother–daughter bonds.

Parent–Child: Benevolence. While family is important in most cultures, the emphasis on loyalty and obligation to the family in Chinese culture is unparalleled. In Chinese folklore and stories of the Confucian tradition, defiance of parental authority results in the admonition, punishment, or death of the transgressor. It is the benevolence of the parents that saves the child and enables them to achieve maturity and independence.

Younger–Elder: Honor. The "younger" or child is expected to honor the elder or parent, as between the parent–child or elder–younger sibling relationships; and the younger is expected to return this kindness in adulthood, which shows mutual dependence between generations.

Elder–Younger: Protection. The parent or elder is expected to protect the "younger," as between the parent–child or elder–younger sibling relationship, and the younger is expected to return this kindness in adulthood, which shows mutual dependence between generations.

ACHIEVING A POSITIVE IDENTITY

People hold differing worldviews, which are influenced by culture and help to shape their identity. The next three lessons are intended to help counselors understand the psyche of Chinese American immigrants from a position of strength. Counselors need to understand dynamic issues from the client's worldview and perspective. The achievement of a positive self and cultural identity needs to be explained from a developmental perspective, not from a pathology or marginal perspective.

Lesson 4. Bicultural Identity

Bondage Messages: "Be American! Being Westernized is modern. Give up traditional ways!"
Bonding Image: Achieve a yin-yang balance in one's identity.
Action: Avoid stereotypic comparisons between cultures. Engage in a bidirectional process to achieve a bicultural identity.

Principle

A Value-Orientation Model suggests that cultures differ in their attitudes and views along dimensions of time, human activity, social relationships, and relationships of people to nature (Ibrahim, 1985). Asian values tend to be family oriented, based on well-defined family roles, an emphasis on family loyalty and obligation, and the primacy of the parent–child bond. Western values, on the other hand, tend to be individual oriented, based on the nuclear family, an emphasis on the husband–wife bond, and the primacy of the marital bond. Asian families emphasize a hierarchical orientation over an egalitarian one in Western families. Within Asian culture, patriarchal principles of Confucianism have been challenged by the matriarchal principles of Taoism in China; this tension is illustrated in the mythology, legends, symbols, and stories discussed in this book.

Consequently, the stereotypical descriptions of Chinese families and Chinese Americans as "traditional" or "modern" are inaccurate. The assumption of a unidirectional process is misleading. Using a position of difference rather than one of comparison between Chinese and American cultures is more likely to minimize negative connotations and pejorative meanings about Chinese cultural behaviors. For example, an authoritarian orientation has negative connotations from a Western perspective; I prefer the term "hierarchical orientation" in describing the Chinese psyche, which views power and authority with benevolence as opposed to something dictatorial. "Suppression of emotions" is another common term to describe Chinese Americans that has negative connotations from a Western perspective. Rather, it is the management of one's emotions versus the expression of one's emotions that is valued in Chinese value. Moreover, private expression of emotion is neither suppressed nor disapproved; it is the public manifestation of emotions that is suppressed by Asians.

Lesson 5. Contradictions of Culture

Bondage Message: "We are all the same."
Bonding Image: Jade Mountain of the west versus Garden of Eden in the east.
Action: Live with the contrasts between Chinese and American cultures. Accept the irrational when contrasting cultural views are placed side by side. This may require denial and splitting in order to maintain the integrity of each; some things cannot be integrated.

Principle

When differing worldviews such as those of Asian and Western cultures come together, they may conflict. In developing their cultural identities, Chinese Americans must achieve a yin-yang balance between the two cultures. It is a dynamic process that does not require that we integrate the two cultural perspectives in order to achieve a positive bicultural identity.

Opposing and contradictory views between Asian and Western cultures transcend virtually all dimensions of interpersonal relationships, family structure, food preferences, and health practices. These are evident in their worldviews, cultural symbols, and cultural practices. While the difference may be one of emphasis, it is significant. To view them as the same marginalizes their importance.

Lesson 6. Immigration Is Traumatic: Loss and Abandonment

Bondage Message: Stay within the confines of the familiar—for example, Chinatowns—that limit and restrict opportunities.
Bonding Image: Phoenix triumphantly rises from the ashes of destruction.
Action: Acknowledge the trauma of immigration and work on how to mourn the losses and resolve abandonment guilt.

Principle

The journey of immigration is traumatic; it is about loss and separation. Feelings of loss and abandonment are common and can result in lifelong suffering. These are developmental tasks and processes. They may be developmental crises; but let's not make them pathological. Many behaviors and practices among Chinese immigrant families are attempts to preserve the cultural vestiges that keep their memories alive. As so much is lost and left behind, we need to translate these behaviors into transformation experiences and journeys—like the phoenix that triumphantly rises from the ashes of destruction.

STORYTELLING: A METHOD OF HEALING

Storytelling is a method that can be used to heal, to grow, and to nurture. The next three lessons are about journey, transformation, and immigration legend, to enable individuals and families to feel empowered and to find their voices.

Lesson 7. Journey of Immigration

Bondage Message: Lift yourself up by your bootstraps. America is the land of equal opportunity for everyone.
Bonding Image: The unbreakable spirit of Monkey King.
Action: Create your own identity culture on the journey to enlightenment.

Principle

Immigration is a journey. In *Journey to the West,* the four travelers need to discover truth from fiction, demons from spirits, and avoid being fooled by appearances. For Chinese American immigrants, race, gender, age, and class pose challenges not unlike the 81 trials faced by Monkey King. The character of Monkey King is similar to the unbreakable spirit of Chinese American immigrants.

Immigrants must survive and create for themselves a new identity in a strange new world. It is a journey that takes them through many transformations of suffering and pain, confusion and anger before they achieve enlightenment at the end of that journey. These transformations, both pathological and adaptive, speak to the many adventures that immigrants have on their way. It is a journey that must be made, one that should not be forgotten; it is a developmental process. Some immigration themes common to most immigrants and their families follow.

Immigration Themes

Fate and Faith: Our Future. It is our faith that sustains us on this journey; or perhaps it is our fate that makes us continue our travels. The symbols of the Golden Mountain, the American Dream, and the Statue of Liberty are there to remind us of why we came, and to wish us speedy passage. Yet many immigrants do get stuck, trapped by the guilt and sadness that bury us in the Golden Mountain of the West. For all immigrants, the task is to restore, to heal, and to bond.

Promise and Obligation. Chinese immigrants leave their families, their culture, and their country behind. The abandonment guilt often leads to lifelong anguish. The obligation to family is also lifelong in the fulfilling of a promise or in the honoring of an elder to repay a debt.

Adoption: Family Lineage. The immigration process often involves psychological issues not unlike those of adoption. All immigrants adopt a culture. They adopt the dress, the behaviors, and the beliefs of the host culture while retaining aspects of their culture of origin. For some, it is just the exterior. For others, it is obliteration of the interior. For still others, it is the bringing together as one, like the yin and the yang.

Impact of Poverty. The impact of poverty on the psyche was significant as the scarcity of resources resulted in favoritism, deprivation, and shame. Even as economic conditions improved among immigrant families, the fear of pity and shame from not having enough to eat was often lifelong—another form of bondage.

Racism: Constant Work and Vigilance. Often perceived as perpetual foreigners, Asian Americans need to be vigilant in evaluating and judging whether they are being responded to because of race and ethnicity. Racism is less overt in today's world. Consequently, Asian Americans run the risk of being overly suspicious or overly sensitive. Asian Americans also have to decide when and if they want to be more ethnic. This too requires constant work and vigilance, an effort that is unnecessary for whites.

Lesson 8. Creating Immigration Legends

Bondage Message: Constrain yourself to conform to expectations, like Chinese women in bound feet.
Bonding Image: Crouching Tiger, Hidden Dragon.
Action: Families need to create their own immigration legend to preserve the memories and build the bonds of family and culture so they will not be forgotten.

Principle

I see images of old Chinese American ladies in knit hats and sweaters, wearing layers of clothing to keep them warm. Their sense of fashion is dark earth-tone colors to be modest, small (but not too flamboyant) multicolor flowery prints to give some life, and sensible shoes to help them make their journey. I see images of old Chinese American men sitting around mahjong tables, telling stories of anguish and struggle—embellishing their stories to ease the pain and lessen the shame.

The oral histories, the letter writing, the travels, and ultimately the stories create the cultural myths, the family bonds, and the immigration legends. Immigrant families work to survive; they live to see the day that their children will fulfill their promise in the new world. Many fear that their children will forget their saga of struggle and suffering.

Open the dragon gates and draw on the cultural symbols to help families to heal. The journey of immigration, the task of survival, and the memories left behind are all part of creating a new identity and bonding. The stories that speak of suffering and strength, of poverty and riches, must be told. It is the bitter that makes us know the sweet. It is the cold that makes us know what is hot. It is the spicy that lets us know what is mild.

Lesson 9. Empowerment and Finding Your Voice

Bondage Message: Like Monkey King, you will be oppressed by the Mountain of Five Fingers.
Bonding Image: Remember Kuan Yin, Goddess of Mercy, hovering over us.
Action: Find your voice.

Principle

We are at the conclusion of the immigration journey. Now that we have reclaimed the past and examined the present, it is time to move toward the future. Just as Monkey King had 81 tasks (or nine times nine, representing longevity and immortality) to test him and had to travel on foot, all immigrants must travel a tedious journey and endure the trials of oppression, acculturation, and poverty, before they reach enlightenment, that is, empowerment.

I started with the voice of my mother; through her eyes, we saw the world and her journey to the West—her struggles, her losses, and her joys. By the age of 84, she had achieved the blessing of having 100 children (including grandchildren, great-grandchildren, nieces, nephews, and their offspring). She was a loving mother. She died tragically in a car accident, suffering in her death as she did in her life. As we went through her effects, we were reminded of how she lived, of how much she gave. There were the gifts she never used because they were too precious to open; the gifts she never gave because there was a tomorrow for her to look forward to. There was unfinished business.

She was frugal with herself until the end; she was generous with others until her death. Our consolation was that she knew she was loved. The scores of people who came to pay their respects at her funeral were testimony to her as a person. She would have felt that her life was worth living. For she had achieved the greatest honor a woman could want—to be respected and appreciated, to be loved by her family. She died as she lived—a martyr and a hero. She often felt insignificant in the world; but she was significant in her life, to her family. We will not forget her journey. This book finishes her story. She has found her voice.

The Future

My Family

Life is full of many wonderful pleasures.
Family is one that is worth more than any priceless treasure.

Together we share experiences that are memorable and fun,
Being one part of the whole links us all as one.
The support and understanding we have for each other,
Is helpful in learning so much from one another.

The unbroken alliance shared with relatives from all over,
Are everlasting friendships, so rare like a three-leaf clover.

My family is special through my eyes that will see,
And they will always mean so much to me.

Tracey Lynette Ong

The number nine in Chinese symbolizes longevity; thus it is appropriate to end this book with nine chapters. Chapter 9 is the chapter yet to
be written. This chapter is for our future and for the generations that
will follow. It is the blank slate for the immigration legend to be continued and created. It is the bond to be sustained through time and
with the family.

Notes

Chapter 2

1. According to Chinese culture, people are born with or without basic elements of metal, wood, wind, water, or fire. Balance of these elements is essential for optimal functioning. The imbalances of water play out in the character of An-Mei.

2. The maternal gift of gold reinforces the generational bonds while also serving to restore the metal balance.

3. The theme of obedience and loyalty of child to parent are major principles of the *Twenty-Four Stories* prescribed by Confucianism.

Chapter 3

1. Chinese Americans often have both an American name and a Chinese name; yet we were often expected to address one another by titles—for example, "elder sister" or "younger sister."

2. Charlie Chan, a Chinese detective played on television in the 1950s, dominated the American image of Chinese Americans.

3. Many Chinese immigrants bought papers and assumed another identity in order to immigrate into the United States.

Chapter 4

1. The grammar in parts of this narrative may appear unusual in that the oral history is translated from the Chinese spoken by my mother, a language with a grammatical and linguistic structure very different from that of English. Romanized versions of Chinese words are followed by their English translation in parentheses; no formal system exists in English to translate Toisanese, which is a village dialect. Years are recorded in the year of the Republic (i.e., Men Guo) and translated into the Gregorian calendar. This was how my mother and many early Toisanese immigrants marked time; it demonstrated their support for the establishment of the Republic of China under President Sun Yat Sen. Names also follow the Chinese Confucian tradition of using honorific titles (rather than their given names) for family, relatives, and honored friends denoting their hierarchical relationship within the maternal or paternal family.

According to Chinese custom, the titles my mother used to talk about family, friends, and relatives were always those that we would use as her children; for example, *Dai Q* is Eldest Maternal Uncle, the only name we used when referring to him.

2. This was how my mother always described her mother. Her lifelong feeling of abandonment was always shrouded in mystery. Yet you saw her pain and felt her loss each time she repeated this.

3. My mother's first cousin, also called Uncle in Chinese.

4. My mother's brother.

5. A dog's life was considered pitiful because they are considered food in China, not pets as it is here in America. My parents would only raise German Shephards because they were considered useful as watchdogs. Whenever our dog misbehaved, my mother would always threaten to cook him; we never did.

6. My mother sponsored Poy Q and his family to come to the United States. They arrived here in the 1980s after a 40-year separation, a common practice among Toisanese immigrants to fulfill their family obligation and debt.

7. Early Toisanese Chinese immigrated to the United States under assumed identities, whose papers they purchased often at great personal and financial risk.

8. We never knew if these descriptions of medical diseases were a poor translation or cultural folklore. This may have been cataract surgery.

9. Year One of the Republic of China. We never really knew if my mother was born 1911 or 1912 since she practiced the Chinese custom of adding a year to her age on January 1 rather than on her birthday. Since she used the lunar calendar and we used the Gregorian calendar, we often could not remember her birthday. Moreover, her "paper" age was 9 years younger than her birth age, confusing us even more.

10. I wondered how my mother, always so nurturing and concerned about others, could be so unsympathetic. I could only conclude that this preserved her view of how her father's utmost concern was for her welfare. This practice was customary in China when women depended on men for their livelihood. Children were a liability especially when food was scarce in a poverty stricken environment.

11. Close friends are called *Ah Seem* (Auntie) or *Ah Sook* (Uncle) to bestow respect and intimacy to the relationship.

12. We did not know this until we were well into adulthood. My mother had kept this secret for many years because the memories drenched up painful emotions of separation, guilt, and abandonment. Following Chinese custom, she counted him among her children. In my youth, my mother's stories were confusing because of gaps in dates and contradictory information about our brother in China. We attributed these to memory lapses or her confusion for details. Only later did we learn that our brother Sel Ming had been a replacement for this first brother who died.

13. I was never clear if my mother believed these omens or if it eased the painful loss. The senseless death of her child associated with my father's killing of the goose was a source of disagreement for years.

14. I had brought these 9 coins to a jeweler when I was about 14 to have them made into a bracelet. When I returned to pick it up, the jeweler showed it to me and dropped it into a bag out of my sight behind the counter. Once outside the store, I was so excited I wanted to see the bracelet again. The bag was empty; I had been conned. I returned to the store; the jeweler denied everything. We could do nothing since I was too young and my mother spoke little English.

15. My mother's obligation and debt to all the Lee and Lau clans was clear though she disagreed with him while he lived over being able to provide financial support on their own meager means. I could sense the resignation in her voice as she recounted how they all starved to death, and wondered if she questioned what her fate would have been if Papa had not gone to *gnoy yerng*.

16. Since villages were organized by clans, every male in the same village was considered a village uncle, denoting a more distant relationship than the other honorific titles accorded to uncles in one's extended family.

17. My parents both recounted this story repeatedly during our childhood with pride and amusement as an indication of my father's strong character; he was brave and a strong advocate of justice against all odds.

18. This was the honorific name given even though there was no blood relationship since we had so few blood relatives in America.

19. My mother's anger over this assault on her virtue resurfaced 60 years later in our trip to Los Angeles where we met members of the Lau clan.

20. The bonds they created were lifelong, as they shared the experience and trauma of fleeing Nanjing together. It was a bond that spanned both continents and almost a half century in time as my mother was not to see them again for almost 40 years.

21. As a result of the war, my mother was often critical of Japanese when she met them in the United States, believing them to be of poor character.

References

Barlow, T. E., with Bjorge, G. J. (Eds.) (1989). *I myself am a woman: Selected writings of Ding Ling.* Boston: Beacon Press.

Bettelheim, B. (1976). *The uses of enchantment: The meaning and importance of fairy tales.* New York: Alfred A. Knopf.

Bierlein, J. F. (1994). *Parallel myths.* New York: Ballantine Books.

Campbell, J. (1949). *Hero with a thousand faces.* Princeton, NJ: Princeton University Press.

Chang, I. (1997). *The rape of Nanking: The forgotten holocaust of World War II.* New York: Penguin.

Chang, I. C. (1968). *Chinese fairy tales.* New York: Schocken Books.

Chin, J. C., Liem, J. H., Ham, M.D-C., & Hong, G. (1993). *Transference and empathy in Asian American psychotherapy: Cultural values and treatment needs* (p. 25). Westport, CT: Praeger.

Confucius. (2004). Available: http://encarta.msn.com/encyclopedia_761551784/Confucius.html Retrieved June 8, 2004.

Confucius and Confucianism. Reacting to the past. (2004). Available: http://beatl.barnard.columbia.edu/reacting/china/confucianism.html# philosophy Retrieved June 8, 2004.

Eng, P. (1999). *Warrior lessons: An Asian American's journey into power.* New York: Pocket Books.

Gibson, C. (1996). *Signs and symbols: An illustrated guide to their meaning and origins.* New York: Barnes & Nobles Books.

Harding, M. E. (1971). *Woman's mysteries: Ancient and modern.* Boston: Shambhala Publications.

The Holy Bible, King James Version. (1999). New York: American Bible Society.

Heuscher, J. E. (1974). *A psychiatric study of myths and fairy tales.* Springfield, IL: Charles C. Thomas.

Ibrahim, F.A. (1985) Effective cross-cultural counseling and psychotherapy: A framework. *The Counseling Psychologist, 12,* 625–638.

Kim, E. H. (1981). Visions and fierce dreams: A commentary on the works of Maxine Hong Kingston. *Amerasia Journal, 8*(2), 145–162.

Kim, J. (1981). The process of Asian American identity development: A study of Japanese-American women's perceptions of their struggle to achieve personal identities as Americans of Asian ancestry. *Dissertation Abstracts International, 42,* 155 1A. (University Microfilms No. 81–18080)

Kingston, M.H. (1989). *The woman warrior: Memoirs of a girlhood among ghosts.* New York: Random House.

Kinkead, G. (1991). *Chinatown: A portrait of a closed society.* New York: HarperCollins.

Koster, H. (Director). (1961). *The flower drum song.* Universal International Pictures.

Kristeva, J. (1986). *About Chinese women.* New York: Marion Boyars.

Lam, A. (1996, March 13). *Drinking tiger soup.* Pacific News Service.

Lee, A. (Director). (2004). *Crouching tiger, hidden dragon.* [Film.] Columbia Tri-Star Studio. ASIN: B00003CXR4.

Lee, E. (1997). *Working with Asian Americans: A guide for clinicians.* New York: The Guilford Press.

Logan, J. (Director). (1957). *Sayonara.* MGM/VA Studios.

Loo, C. M., & Yu, C. Y. (1984). Pulse on San Francisco's Chinatown: Health service utilization and health status. *Amerasia, 11*(1), 55–73.

Lucas, G. (Director). (1977). *Star wars.* Lucasfilm Ltd.

Luo Guanzhong. *Romance of the three kingdoms.* Available: http://www.3kingdoms.net/intro.htm Retrieved May 2002.

McDermott, J. F., & Lum, K. Y. (1980) Star wars: The modern developmental fairy tale. *Bulletin of the Menninger Clinic, 44*(4), 381–390.

Mencius. (1895). *The Chinese classics. Vol II: The works of Mencius* (J. Lagge, Trans.). Oxford: Clarendon Press.

Nahm, H.Y. (2003). *Suzy Wong revisited.* Available: http://goldsea.com/Personalities/Kwannancy/kwannancy.html. Retrieved 2003.

Puccini, G. (Composer). (1904). *Madame Butterfly.* Available: http://www.culturevulture.net/Opera/Butterfly.htm. Retrieved June 2002.

Quine, R. (Director). (1960). *The world of Suzie Wong.* Paramount Studios.

Schönberg, C-M., Maltby, R., & Boublil, A. (1990). *Miss Saigon.* Milwaukee, WI: Hal Leonard Publishing Corporation.

Scott, D. H. (1980). *Chinese popular literature and the child.* Chicago: American Library Association.

Simpson, C. S. (2001, March 23). Crouching tiger: The rebirth of myth. *The Chronicle of Higher Education,* B19.

Stepanchuck, S., & Wong, C. (1991). *Mooncakes and hungry ghosts: Festivals of China.* San Francisco: China Books & Periodicals.

Sue, D. W., & Carter, R. T. (1998). *Multicultural counseling competencies: Individual and organizational development.* Thousand Oaks, CA: Sage.

Sue, S., & Sue, D. W. (1971). Chinese American personality and mental health. *Amerasia Journal, 1,* 36–49.

Tan, A. (1989). *Joy luck club.* New York: McGraw-Hill College.

Tseng, W-S., & Hsu, J. (1972). The Chinese attitude toward parental authority as expressed in Chinese children's stories. *Archives of General Psychiatry, 20,* 28–34.

Wu Ch'eng-en. (1500–1582). *Monkey king.* Available: http://www.china-on-site.com/pages/comic/comiccatalog1.php Retrieved May 2002.

Yu, L. (1974a). *Chinese women in history and legend: Volume 1.* New York: A.R.T.S.

Yu, L. (1974b). *Chinese women in history and legend: Volume 2.* New York: A.R.T.S.

Index

About the Author

Jean Lau Chin, Ed.D., ABPP is Systemwide Dean of the California School of Professional Psychology at Alliant International University. She is a licensed psychologist with over 30 years of clinical, educational, and management experience in health and mental health services. She has held the positions of President for CEO Services, Regional Director for the Massachusetts Behavioral Health Partnership, Executive Director for the South Cove Community Health Center, and Co-Director for the Thom Child Guidance Clinic. She has also been Associate Professor at Boston University School of Medicine and Assistant Professor at Tufts University School of Medicine. Dr. Chin has published and presented in the areas of cultural competent service delivery, ethnic minority, Asian American, and women's issues in health and mental health. Her recent works include a four-volume series on the psychology of prejudice and discrimination, and an upcoming book on feminist leadership, based on her presidential initiative for the Society for the Psychology of Women of the American Psychological Association.